WHITEWATER COOKS

with friends

Thanks to the owners of Whitewater Ski Resort: Dean Prodan, Mitch Putnam, Andrew Kyle.

To all our recipe contributers, we thank you and hope that you keep sharing:

Tana Tocher, Sheri Weichel, Blake Covernton, Daphne Van Alstine, Mary Ellen Mcknight, Gail Morrison, Annie Bailey, Barb Gosney, Jane Quennell, Jann Galliver, Laura Gregor-Lundy, Lisa Pantages, Liz Abraham, Linda Klein, Margie Rosling, Marilyn Kopansky, Mia Fujibayashi, Michele Repine, Michelle Shumay, Mike Adams, Monica Hoffman, Nathan Fong, David Lewis, Sue Lamb, Pauline Riley, Pat McLaughlin, Sean Hetherington, Bernice Hetherington, Shelley Sorensen, Anita Sorensen, Susi Donaldson, Ralf Dauns, Jean Francois Plante, Marianne Batty, Marcia Hetherington, Kim Irving, Petra Lehman, Barb Tocher, Cathy Tocher.

Thanks to our beautiful models:

David Hernandez, Brian Monroe, Cheryl Link, Ali Adams, Conner Adams, Maya Abraham, Tashi Neary, Dawson Abraham, Mitchell McCallum, Sue McLaughlin, Nikko Fujibayashi-Lazier, Grace McLaughlin, Nadja Hall, Mya McLaughlin, and Tempy.

Much thanks to our proofers:

Kristine Huiberts, Peter Lamb, Mike Adams, Conner Adams, Ali Adams

And to Cottonwood Kitchens, Maison, Jacqueline Costa, Cheryl Link and Enso Hair Design for their support.

ISBN 978-0-9811424-1-8

Recipe Development/Design: Shelley Adams, Marianne Abraham
Food Styling and Recipe Testing: Shelley Adams, Marianne Abraham, Emmy McKnight
Writing and Editing: Shelley Adams and Marianne Abraham
Design and Layout: Minn Benedict, Prefix Media - www.prefixmedia.com
Photography: David R. Gluns
Back Cover Text: Nancy Wise
Inside Flap Text: Kristine Huiberts
Introduction: Margie Rosling, Shelley Adams, Ali Adams
Additional Photographs by: Megan Salcak
Submitted Contributor Photographs: Bernice, Nathan, Jane, Cathy, Barbie, Marcia, Fiona, Michele, Gail

Published by Alicon Holdings Ltd., Nelson BC

Printed and bound in Canada by Friesens Book Division

To find out where you can purchase the series of *Whitewater Cooks*, visit www.whitewatercooks.com

dedicated to friends & family everywhere

so you always have our favourite recipes in one place.

contents

food, for me, is all about sharing.

Sharing ambience, flavours, ingredients, conversation, wine, laughter and of course, recipes.

When Mike and I owned Whitewater Ski Resort, I ran the Fresh Tracks Café and the skiers were constantly begging for the recipes. So with the prompting of my friend Lori McGinnis, I decided to accommodate their wishes and write a cookbook. I thought that after *Whitewater Cooks, Pure, Simple and Real* was published, my career as a cookbook author would be over. But out-of-town fans and Nelsonites thought differently and were again asking when the second book was coming. Thus was born the second book, *Whitewater Cooks at Home*.

Once again I thought my little career as a cookbook author was over and I had shared all I had to share. Each time that I was encouraged to compile recipes for a third book, my answer was a polite "I don't think so". After all, Mike and I had just retired and were looking forward to our new adventures.

However, over a great dinner last fall my wise daughter Ali and my very enthusiastic friend Margie reminded me of my mantra...

"great recipes are meant to be shared!"

We tossed around the idea of combining more great recipes from Nelson friends, friends from afar and from my personal collection.

I mentioned the idea of a third book to my longtime friend and catering partner Marianne Abraham and she exclaimed eagerly "I'll help!"

Then I called my incredible team of Dave Gluns and Minn Benedict with the plan and their response was, "What took you so long?!"

So the result of the dinner last fall with my daughter and friend, together with many hours with Marianne writing, testing and tweaking recipes has resulted in *Whitewater Cooks with Friends*.

What this collection of recipes demonstrates is cooking great meals doesn't have to be time consuming or complicated and you don't need to be a trained chef to make fabulous, healthy and delicious food. These recipes can be prepared with ingredients most of us stock in our fridges and cupboards and can be made in a short amount of time if you have done a little bit of planning and prep beforehand. All of the friends who have contributed recipes for this cookbook are amazing home cooks and some have owned a catering company, cooked for ski lodges, catered in the movie business or have worked as chefs in restaurants. They all lead very active, full and happy lives and make wonderful food.

Although they don't all know each other, they share one thing in common with each other and me... love of food and a heartfelt belief in the comforting and nurturing value of delicious meals with family and friends.

When I started Fresh Tracks Café at Whitewater Ski Resort, I had no idea that it would lead to three cookbooks. I have loved creating these books and hope that you get as much joy from these recipes as my friends and I do. For me cooking is a way of life and celebrating my belief that...

every day is a bonus!

7

starters

spiced pear and stilton tarte with mustard cream

Crispy, fresh and rich, this marriage of texture and taste takes the classic combination of fruit and cheese a step above!

serves 4-6

ingredients

mustard cream
6 tbsp whipping cream
3 tbsp grainy dijon mustard
1 $\frac{1}{2}$ tbsp regular dijon
1 tbsp fresh lemon juice
1 tbsp honey

pear tarte
$\frac{1}{2}$ package puff pastry, defrosted and rolled
  on a flour dusted work surface, into a 10
  inch square*
1 egg, beaten with 1 tbsp milk (egg wash)
1 large, firm but ripe pear, halved lengthwise
  and cored
1 tbsp olive oil
$\frac{1}{3}$ tsp cayenne pepper
2 cups baby arugula
4 oz crumbled stilton or goat cheese

*if you want to use the whole package of
puff pastry, just double the recipe.

method

Whisk all mustard cream ingredients together in a small bowl. Season with salt and pepper and set aside.

Preheat oven to 375°.
Place pastry on a parchment lined baking sheet.
Score the pastry by cutting only halfway through, around its entire edge with a sharp knife, to make a $\frac{1}{2}$ inch border.
Brush the border with the egg wash.
Fold the edges up at the score line and crimp with a fork.
Brush this new edge with more eggwash.
Cut pear halves vertically into thin slices and toss with olive oil and cayenne pepper.
Scatter arugula over puff pastry sheet.
Top with pear slices and then cheese.
Place in lower third of oven and bake for about 25 minutes until cheese is melted and pastry is crisp and brown.
Remove from oven, place on cutting board and cut into eight pieces.
Drizzle with room temperature mustard cream.

You can assemble this whole appetizer and take it to your party location. Just make sure it's kept cool and then pop it in the oven at your destination. Serve warm, right out of the oven.

prosciutto wrapped scallops with basil aioli and honeydew

Needing an easy appetizer one evening on our way to Emmy and Blake's, we stopped at the Fisherman's Market and bought some fresh and beautiful Digby scallops. "Bacon wrapped" sprang to mind, which evolved into prosciutto…that in turn, evoked images of the classic Melon Wrapped in Prosciutto, and that's how it all came together. It's like having two appetizers in one!

serves 6

ingredients

basil aioli
1 cup good quality mayonnaise
2 tbsp whipping cream
1 cup fresh basil, chopped coarsely
1 garlic clove, crushed
½ lemon, juice of
½ tsp salt
½ tsp pepper

18 bamboo skewers, soaked in water for at
  least an hour
6 large slices prosciutto, cut into lengthwise
  strips wide enough to cover each scallop
18 Digby or large scallops, fresh if possible
2 cups spicy greens
1 honeydew melon, peeled and thinly sliced

method

Combine all aioli ingredients with a hand-held mixing wand or food processor until smooth.
Place in a plastic squeeze bottle.

Lay prosciutto strips on a work surface.
Place a scallop on each strip and wrap up tightly.
Insert one scallop on each skewer, leaving the scallop at the end of the skewer.
Grill scallops on pre-heated barbeque until they are just done and prosciutto is getting brown and crispy, about 3 minutes per side.
Place spicy greens on serving platter and lay the skewers of scallops around the edge.
Mound the honeydew slices in the middle of the platter.
Drizzle basil aioli all over scallop skewers.

This is pretty easy, eh? Cantaloupe or papaya works well in place of honeydew.

crostini with beef tenderloin, cambozola & horseradish crème fraiche

There's nothing like this appetizer of tender beef, horseradish, fresh tomatoes and arugula to satisfy even the most famished guest until the "real dinner" is served. Full of protein, it's the perfect complement to a potluck table dominated by chips and salsa.

serves 5-6

ingredients

one 1 lb piece of beef tenderloin
2 tbsp soy sauce
2 tbsp olive oil
¼ cup white wine vinegar
2 tbsp salt
8 oz cambozola cheese, room temperature
2 tbsp butter, room temperature
¼ cup horseradish
½ cup sour cream
¼ cup whipping cream
½ tsp salt
2 cups arugula
1 pint cherry tomatoes, halved, or small
  tomatoes, sliced
1 baguette (for crostini)
olive oil
3 peeled garlic cloves cut in half
¼ cup olive oil
½ cup capers

method

Whisk together soy sauce, olive oil and vinegar, and pour over beef.
Cover and marinate for at least an hour or overnight.
Remove beef from marinade, sprinkle with salt and sear in a hot pan on all sides until nicely browned.
Finish cooking in a preheated 375° oven for another 15 minutes for medium rare beef.
Let cool completely and slice thinly.
Mash together cambozola cheese and butter with a fork.
Mix together horseradish, sour cream, whipping cream and salt with a whisk and put in a squeeze bottle.
Slice baguette into 12-18 pieces, brush with olive oil on both sides and toast in 350° oven until golden brown.
Remove from oven and rub with a halved garlic clove.
Heat olive oil over medium heat and fry capers until crisp, about 3 minutes.
Arrange the toasted baguette slices on a large platter.
Spread each crostini with the cambozola butter.
Lay on a few arugula leaves and top with a slice of cooled beef and a cherry tomato half or tomato slice.
Drizzle the horseradish mixture over the crostinis and top with a bit of fresh ground pepper and crispy capers.

If there isn't a worthy tomato available, replace the fresh cherry tomatoes with a few julienned sun-dried tomatoes. We always use the ones packed in oil. Fancy roast beef sandwiches anyone?

jann's grilled asparagus wraps with crema di balsamico

Jann is another one of Nelson's busy women who is also a fabulous cook. We all love eating quick to prepare, good food, so that's why we appreciate recipes like this one! Easy to make, take and fling on anyone's barbeque; it can be an appetizer or a side dish with just about any entree.

serves 6

ingredients

24 asparagus spears (depending on
  thickness), about 3-4 spears per wrap
6 thin slices of prosciutto
6 thin slices of fontina cheese
Crema di Balsamico*

*available at Railway Station Specialty Meats and Deli in Nelson and Ferrarro Foods in Rossland, or at your favourite speciality food store.

method

Preheat barbeque to medium heat.
Bring a pot of water to a boil and quickly cook the asparagus until just bright green. Then plunge the asparagus into cold water to stop cooking.
Drain and wrap asparagus in paper towels.
Place prosciutto slices on working surface.
Lay a slice of fontina cheese on top of each slice of prosciutto.
Lay asparagus spears on top of cheese and roll up tightly.
Insert a toothpick through each roll to hold it together while grilling.
Brush barbeque with oil and grill until proscuittto is browned and crisp and cheese just begins to melt, about 2 minutes per side.
Remove toothpicks and place on platter or individual plates.
Drizzle with Crema di Balsamico and serve.

Sounds too easy to be true, but that...is a good thing!

pacific sashimi towers

This exquisite appetizer repeatedly lured us to a small upcountry restaurant in Maui. We have redefined it to include our own B.C. coastal delicacies. Don't be dissuaded by the many steps in this recipe. The fun of creating it is worth the effort. Eating it is even better...

serves 6

ingredients

¾ lb in total, sashimi grade tuna*
  (¼ lb sliced for sashimi slices and ½ lb
  finely chopped for tartare)
¼ lb smoked salmon lox (12 slices)
6 cups spicy greens
½ cup sliced pickled ginger, for garnish
1 tbsp tobiko (flying fish roe) for garnish*

wontons
24 wonton wrappers (Mandarin brand are
  best)
2 cups vegetable oil

wasabi dressing
2 tbsp rice vinegar
2 tbsp soy sauce
½ cup olive oil
1 tbsp prepared wasabi paste, out of the tube
2 tsp sesame seeds, toasted

tartare layer
2 tbsp good quality mayonnaise
1 tsp chili garlic sauce
2 tbsp green onions, chopped
2 tsp tobiko (flying fish roe)
1 tbsp fresh cilantro, chopped
½ pound of the tuna, finely chopped

avocado salsa
1 large avocado, finely diced
1 tbsp honey
½ lime, juice of
2 tbsp cilantro, chopped

*available at the Fisherman's Market.

method

Heat one cup of oil in frying pan and when just about smoking, fry half of the wontons for about 8 seconds per side or until just golden brown. Drain them on paper towel and set aside.
Discard this oil and repeat process with the remaining oil and wontons.

Combine all wasabi dressing ingredients in a small food processor or blender and mix until sesame seeds are slightly ground. Place in a squeeze bottle.

Combine mayonnaise, chili garlic sauce, green onions, tobiko and cilantro. Add the chopped tuna and stir lightly to make the tartare.

Mix avocado salsa ingredients together lightly in a small bowl.

Arrange one cup of spicy greens on a serving plate.
Place a wonton on the greens, then one spoonful of the tartare mix, then another wonton, then two slices of the smoked salmon lox, then another wonton, then two slices of the tuna sashimi, then another wonton and finish with one spoonful of the avocado salsa.
Drizzle with wasabi dressing.
Garnish with pickled ginger and tobiko.

An additional layer of mango or papaya salsa makes this tower even more spectacular. The best way to eat this is to smash through the entire tower with a knife and fork, mixing it together a bit to blend the flavours.

mesa plate...or 3 great things to serve with cheese

Have these three great compotes in your fridge to pair them with some delectable cheeses and our Roasted Tapas Nuts (on page 30) to create our Mesa Plate.

ingredients

fig jam
(makes 4 cups)

2 cups dried figs, stems
  removed, chopped
  coarsely
2 1/2 cups water
1 orange, juice and zest of
1/2 cup honey
3 tbsp red wine vinegar
1 cinnamon stick
1 tsp fresh ginger, peeled
  and finely grated
1/2 tsp salt
1 tbsp olive oil
2 shallots, finely chopped
1 clove garlic, crushed
1/2 cup walnuts, toasted
  and chopped

fiona's eggplant pickle
(makes 3 cups)

1/2 cup vegetable oil
1/2 tsp dried chili flakes
4 tbsp garlic, crushed
3 tbsp fresh ginger, peeled
  and finely chopped
2 tbsp mustard seeds
1 1/2 tsp turmeric
3 tsp garam masala
1 large eggplant, cubed
  into 1/2 inch pieces (about
  3 cups)
1 1/2 tsp salt
1/2 cup brown sugar
3/4 cup white vinegar
1/2 tsp sambal oelek (ground
  chili paste)

summer peach chutney
(makes about 6 cups)

2 1/2 pounds peaches,
  blanched, peeled, pitted and
  chopped into 3/4 inch pieces
  (about 4 cups)
1 tbsp vegetable oil
1 medium onion, finely
  chopped
2 garlic cloves, crushed
2 cups apple cider vinegar
1 cup brown sugar
1 cup sultana raisins
1 tsp fresh red chili pepper,
  seeded and finely chopped
2 tsp fresh ginger, minced
4 whole star anise
1 tsp salt
1 tsp cinnamon
1 tsp coriander
1 tsp turmeric
1/4 tsp allspice

to see method, go to page 22.

method

fig jam

Soak figs in water, juice and zest of orange in a heavy bottomed saucepan for half an hour.

Slowly heat this mixture to medium heat and add honey, vinegar, cinnamon stick, ginger and salt.

Simmer at a low boil for 20 minutes, stirring occasionally, until liquid is reduced and fig mixture thickens.

Heat olive oil in a sauté pan on medium heat, cook shallots and garlic until soft and translucent, and add to fig mixture.

Add chopped walnuts to fig mixture and cook to meld flavours – about 5 minutes.

Remove cinnamon stick and whiz with a hand-held mixing wand until jam-like.

Let cool and store in glass jars in the fridge for up to 1 month.

fiona's eggplant pickle

Heat oil in a heavy bottomed saucepan to low medium heat.

Add chili flakes, garlic, ginger, mustard seeds, turmeric and garam masala and sauté for 3 minutes until your whole kitchen smells like an Indian spice market.

Add cubed eggplant and cook until soft, about 5 minutes on medium heat.

Add salt, sugar and vinegar and stir to combine.

Simmer, stirring occasionally, reducing liquid for 15 minutes on low heat.

Remove from heat and stir in sambal oelek.

Let cool and store in a glass jar in fridge for up to one month.

summer peach chutney

Heat oil in large, heavy bottomed stockpot over low medium heat.

Add onion and garlic and sauté for 3 minutes or until tender.

Transfer onion mixture to large bowl and add cider vinegar, brown sugar, raisins, chili pepper, ginger, star anise, salt, cinnamon, coriander, turmeric and allspice and mix well.

Add the chopped peaches to onion mixture, in the same large bowl and combine well.

Return all ingredients to same large stockpot, bring to a boil, reduce heat and simmer for 1 hour until thickened, stirring frequently.

Ladle chutney into glass jars and store in fridge for up to one month.

To the benefit of everyone, the last few years have heralded the rebirth of local, organic cheeses and some of the best cheeses can be found right in this region.

Some of our favourite tasty cheeses* to pair with the Mesa Plate compotes are Poplar Grove Double Crème Camembert (from Penticton), Naramata Blue Bench (from Naramata), Organic Rocky Mountain Sharp Cheddar (from Calgary), and Kootenay Alpine Cheese aged Nostrala (from Creston).

Of course, there are fabulous cheeses from all over the world that would take a whole book to fill, so try some recommendations from your local deli as well!

*all available at the Kootenay Co-op.

seafood raviolis with lemongrass sauce

Great for New Years Eve! After all of the rich food during the holiday season, these "dimsum-ish" steamed raviolis make a nice light change. Using a chinese bamboo steamer, readily available at Wing's Grocery, is really the best way to steam them.

makes 40 individual raviolis

ingredients

sauce
1 1/2 tbsp butter
1 medium onion, finely chopped
2 whole lemongrass stalks, sliced into 2 inch
  pieces or 4 tsp lemongrass paste
2 tbsp flour
3 cups whipping cream
1 1/2 tbsp fresh lime juice
1 tsp pepper
1 tsp saffron
3/4 tsp sugar
2 tsp lobster paste** (optional)
salt to taste, if omitting lobster paste

**available at Railway Station Specialty Meats and Deli.

raviolis
80 wonton wrappers (you will use 2 per ravioli)
1 egg yolk mixed with 1/2 cup of water (egg
  wash)
8 oz prawns, peeled and deveined
8 oz scallops
6 oz crabmeat
1 bunch green onions, chopped finely
1/2 tsp pepper
3/4 cup of the lemongrass sauce

paprika and sliced green onions (for garnish)

Because this is such a large recipe, just freeze them, layered with parchment or wax paper in an air tight container. Steam them from frozen, increasing your steaming time to 8-9 minutes.

method

Melt butter in small heavy bottomed saucepan and sauté onion and lemongrass over medium heat until translucent.
Add flour, whisk well and cook for 3 minutes, stirring constantly.
Add whipping cream, stirring until sauce begins to thicken (about 8-10 minutes).
Turn heat down to low and whisk in lime juice, pepper, saffron, sugar and lobster paste, if using.
Simmer for 1/2 hour, whisking frequently.
Turn heat off, remove lemongrass pieces with a slotted spoon and set aside.

Chop prawns and scallops in food processor until just chunky, or chop by hand on a cutting board.
Transfer to large bowl and add crabmeat, green onions, pepper and 3/4 cup of the lemongrass sauce.
Mix gently until sauce just coats seafood.
Make six raviolis at a time. Start by laying six wontons on a working surface.
Place 1 tbsp of seafood mixture in the middle of each wonton.
Eggwash edges of wontons.
Lay another six wontons on top and crimp sides together with a fork. Make sure edges are sealed well.
Trim square edges off each ravioli to make it round, making sure you leave the crimped edge intact.
Lay crimped raviolis on a baking sheet and cover with plastic film to keep them from drying out.
Repeat process with remaining wontons.
Refrigerate, well covered, for up to 2 hours.
Place the bamboo steamer over a wok or large pot of lightly boiling water, making sure water does not hit the bottom of the steamer.
Place raviolis in steamer, making sure they don't touch each other, with the lid on, and steam in batches for 5-6 minutes.
Remove from steamer, place on a serving platter or individual plates and drizzle with the remaining lemongrass sauce.
Garnish with a sprinkle of paprika and sliced green onions or fresh chives.

bodega style brie on the barbeque

On a chilly fall night, camping on Hornby Island, with limited ingredients in our cooler and a desire for something warm, we came up with this simple starter to graze on while preparing the rest of our dinner. Of course, you can bake this in the oven, but it seems more romantic to do it on the barbeque in the great outdoors!

serves 6-8

ingredients

one 8 inch round of goat or regular brie
1 whole head of garlic, top sliced off
1 tbsp olive oil
2 cups arugula
1 cup fresh basil, julienned
1/2 cup pine nuts, toasted
4 roma tomatoes, diced
2 tbsp capers
2 tbsp olive oil

method

Preheat barbeque to medium low temperature.
Place garlic on a piece of tin foil, large enough to completely wrap garlic.
Drizzle with olive oil and wrap into a tented package.
Place on heated barbeque or 350° oven for 1/2 hour.
Remove from heat, but leave wrapped while cooling, about 10 minutes.
Squeeze garlic flesh out of the skins into a small bowl and mash with a fork.
Scrape "skin" off the top of the brie.
Place brie in heat proof casserole dish or pan.
Spread with the roasted garlic, then the arugula, basil, pine nuts, chopped tomatoes and capers on top of the brie.
Drizzle with olive oil.
Place pan on barbeque and heat until cheese just begins to soften, about 15 minutes, depending on how cold it is outside.
Serve right out of the pan it was barbequed in with fresh baguettes or crackers.

If you can't find an 8 inch round of goat brie, you can also use two 4 inch wheels of goat brie, available at the Kootenay Co-op.

sliced tuna loin with nori strips

If you are looking for a fresh, fast and healthy protein-loaded appetizer, try this one. It is another of Blake's masterpieces that is an easy intro to working with raw tuna, if you've ever been intimidated by that idea. A dish for all ages to easily make and enjoy.

serves 6

ingredients

1 albacore tuna loin (about 1 $\frac{1}{2}$ lbs), frozen*
$\frac{1}{2}$ cup low sodium soy sauce
1 tsp wasabi paste (or to taste)
2 tbsp sesame seeds, toasted
1 package toasted nori strips**

*available at the Fisherman's Market.
**available at the Kootenay Co-op and
Ellison's Market.

method

Remove tuna loin from freezer 3 hours before serving and place in fridge.
Whisk together soy sauce and wasabi.
Slice tuna loin, while still slightly frozen, into $\frac{1}{2}$ inch slices.
Place on a long narrow serving dish.
Drizzle soy and wasabi mix over the tuna slices.
Sprinkle with sesame seeds.
Serve the toasted nori strips in a separate dish on the side.
Fold a nori strip around a slice of the tuna and savour the flavour!

You could also serve the tuna with crispy wontons as they appear in our Pacific Sashimi Towers on page 18.

roasted tapas nuts

We make a big batch of these before the Christmas holidays and store them in a large jar. Serve them with chilled Prosecco wine...and voila! You have an instant tapa when friends unexpectedly drop by.

makes 5 cups

ingredients

2 cups whole almonds, roasted*
1 cup cashews, roasted*
1 cup whole pecans, roasted*
1 cup hazelnuts, roasted and skins off*
1 tbsp olive oil
2 tbsp shallots, sliced in thin rings
3 cloves garlic, peeled and sliced
2 tbsp butter
¼ cup fresh rosemary, finely chopped
¼ tsp cayenne pepper
1 tbsp dark brown sugar
1 tbsp sea salt

method

Preheat oven to 350°.
Place all nuts in a large bowl.
Heat oil in saucepan and sauté shallots until crispy, about 5 minutes.
Add garlic, sauté for another 3 minutes and set aside.
Melt the butter and pour over the nuts.
Add the shallots, garlic, rosemary, cayenne, brown sugar and sea salt.
Mix well, return nuts to the baking sheet and toast for another 8-10 minutes.
Let cool and store in a large glass jar or resealable plastic bags.

Roasting all these nuts takes about 10-12 minutes in a 350° oven.

These sweet and savoury nuts could be included in our "Mesa Plate", found on page 20.

prawns saganaki

While in Greece, Mike and I could not get enough of this delicious appetizer. It was slightly different in every restaurant but was basically just fresh prawns, ripe tomatoes, fresh herbs and feta cheese all baked in the oven until hot and bubbly. Served with warm pita bread, we were in heaven as we shared this flavour filled dish under the olive trees sitting by the turquoise sea. Create this dish and recreate your own scene wherever you are…

serves 4-6

ingredients

1 kg prawns, thawed peeled and head and tails off (B.C. spot prawns are best)
3 tbsp olive oil
1 onion, thinly sliced
4 cloves garlic, crushed
1 red pepper, thinly sliced
1 yellow pepper, thinly sliced
½ tsp chili flakes
6 medium tomatoes, diced
½ cup ouzo
½ cup fresh basil, chopped
1 tsp oregano
1 tsp pepper
1 tsp salt
1 lemon, juice of
½ cup goat feta cheese, crumbled
1 cup saganaki cheese* or mozzarella, grated

1 package pita bread, heated in tin foil in the
    oven for 15 minutes, and cut into quarters

*available at Railway Station Specialty Meats and Deli.

method

Heat oil in oven proof wok or sauté pan.
Add onion, garlic, red and yellow peppers and sauté until just soft, about 5 minutes.
Add chili flakes and tomatoes and sauté for another 2-3 minutes.
Add ouzo and cook until slightly reduced and thick, about 10 minutes.
Add basil, oregano, pepper, salt and lemon juice and stir to combine.
Place prawns in sauce, stir to just combine them and mix in the crumbled feta cheese.
Top with the grated saganaki cheese.
Place wok or oven proof sauté pan in a 350° oven for 15-20 minutes or until prawns have turned pink and cheese is slightly melted.
Remove from oven, set on a cutting board and serve right out of the baking dish surrounded by warm pita bread and kalamata olives.

For the best tomatoes in town, stop by Flexy's fruit stand.

roasted garlic, rosemary potato, artichoke and feta pizza

There are no tomatoes in sight on this somewhat unusual pizza and you will be pleasantly surprised at this delicious flavour combination.

makes two 12 inch round pizzas

ingredients

1 lb unpeeled red potatoes (3-4 medium size) very thinly sliced
2 tbsp fresh rosemary, chopped
1 tsp sea salt
½ tsp pepper
¼ cup olive oil
½ lemon, juice of
4 garlic cloves, crushed

1 tsp instant dry yeast
¼ tsp sugar
¾ cup water, lukewarm
1 ¾ cups flour
½ tsp salt
2 tbsp olive oil (for spreading on dough)

2 whole garlic bulbs, roasted and mashed (see method in bodega brie on page 26)
1 ½ cups marinated artichoke hearts, quartered
¼ tsp chili flakes
1 cup feta cheese, crumbled
1 ½ cups mozzarella, grated

method

Preheat oven to 350°.
Toss potato slices, rosemary, salt, pepper, olive oil, lemon juice and garlic together in large bowl until potato slices are evenly coated.
Spread onto two parchment lined baking sheets, making sure potato slices are in a single layer.
Roast for 20-25 minutes until potato slices are tender and golden and then let cool.

Mix yeast, sugar and water together in a measuring cup.
Stir and let sit for 8 minutes.
Combine flour and salt in a large bowl.
Pour yeast mixture over flour and, using your hands or a wooden spoon, combine until a ragged dough is formed.
Remove from bowl and work into a loose ball on a lightly floured work surface.
Knead well for 2 minutes, turning dough often.
Divide into two equal pieces and shape each one into a 12 inch round.
Place on pizza pan, stone or parchment lined baking sheet.
Spread 1 tbsp of olive oil evenly on to each round.

Preheat oven heat to 500°.
Spread mashed roasted garlic onto pizza dough, then top with roasted potato slices.
Arrange artichoke hearts on top of potato slices and sprinkle with chili flakes.
Sprinkle with feta cheese and finish with mozzarella.
Bake for 15-20 minutes, in the top third of the oven, or until cheese is bubbling and pizza bottom is golden brown.

daph's crunchy salad rolls

Salad rolls burst on to the scene about a decade ago, but they are still around because they are so delicious and healthy. Here is the version that the exuberant and adorably uninhibited Daph regularly serves at her annual all-girl, early evening dance parties!

serves 6-7

ingredients

dipping sauce
1 full recipe, orchid lime salad dressing (found on page 60)
½ cup sweet chili sauce

spring rolls
½ of a 250g package rice vermicelli noodles
1 cup carrot, grated
1 cup bean sprouts, lightly chopped
½ cup long english cucumber, julienned
½ cup green onion, chopped
½ cup fresh mint, finely chopped
½ cup cilantro, finely chopped
2 tsp sesame oil
14 six inch rice paper wrappers*
chopped peanuts, cilantro or green onions, for garnish

*available at Wings Grocery Store and the Kootenay Co-op.

method

Place rice vermicelli noodles in a large bowl, cover completely with boiling water and soak until tender, about 4 minutes.
Drain in a colander, rinse with cold water and let sit for 5 minutes, until completely drained.
Mix noodles with ⅓ of the orchid lime salad dressing.
Chop noodles coarsely and place them in a large bowl, together with carrots, bean sprouts, cucumbers, green onions, mint, cilantro and sesame oil.

Fill a shallow lasagna-type pan with warm water.
Completely submerge two rice paper wrappers.
Remove one wrapper when tender and pliable, after about 15 seconds, and lay carefully on a working surface.
Immediately slide another wrapper under the other one in the water. From now on, every time you pull a wrapper out, slide another one in.
Lay ¼ cup of noodle filling near the edge of the wrapper closest to you, in a log shape.
Roll wrapper around filling once and then tuck edges of wrapper into your roll.
Keep rolling as tightly as possible and then lay seam side down on a plate.
Keep finished rolls covered with a damp tea towel while you are making the remainder.
Arrange on a large platter, garnish and serve with bowls of the orchid lime dipping sauce and sweet chili sauce.

The temperature of the water for softening the rice paper wrappers should only be warm. Boiling water will "cook" the wrappers, causing them to split. Warming up the water in between wrappers will keep your soaking time consistent.

sesame tofu coins

This delicious and easy appetizer will fill up your vegetarian friends and maybe even convert die hard carnivores.

makes 16 coins - serves 8

ingredients

1 carrot, grated
1 egg, beaten
3 tbsp fresh cilantro, chopped
2 tbsp hoisin sauce
2 tsp sesame oil
1 tsp sambal oelek (ground chili paste)
1 tsp salt
one 400g package extra firm tofu, grated
   (about 4 cups)
¾ cup flour
2 tbsp vegetable oil

sauce
¼ cup rice wine vinegar
1 tbsp hoisin sauce
¼ cup sweet chili sauce
½ tsp sesame oil

method

Squeeze excess moisture from grated carrot with your hands and place in large bowl.
Add beaten egg, cilantro, hoisin sauce, sesame oil, sambal oelek and salt and combine.
Add grated tofu into mixture.
Stir in 4 tbsp of the flour and mix well.
Form coins by using 2 tbsp of mixture patted into 2 inch rounds.
Heat oil in sauté pan to medium heat.
Dip each coin into remaining flour and sauté until golden, about 2 minutes per side.

Whisk all sauce ingredients together in a small mixing bowl.
Serve tofu coins on a bed of greens and drizzle with the sauce.

Make these coins a bit bigger and serve them with our Ancient Grains Salad, on page 70, as hearty, healthy lunch.

marilyn's steamed clams

Among the many happy memories of summer days on Hornby Island is one of the hours spent foraging for perfect little butter clams. Long time Helliwell dweller and dear friend Marilyn shares her simple and delicious recipe for straight-up clams.

serves 8-10

ingredients

10 lbs fresh clams, cleaned
¼ cup olive oil
¼ cup butter
3 medium tomatoes, diced
1 medium onion, diced
6 cloves garlic, crushed
2 lemons, juice of
2 cups dry white wine
1 cup italian parsley, chopped for garnish

method

Melt olive oil and butter together in wide-based braising pot.
Sauté tomatoes, onion and garlic until soft.
Add lemon juice and white wine.
Heat until just boiling.
Drop clams in, discarding any open ones first.
Cover and cook until all the clams are open (about 15 to 20 minutes)
Serve in big bowls in the broth with fresh baguette slices on the side for dipping.
Discard any clams that didn't open.

If you are harvesting your own clams, cover them in fresh water and add a handful of oatmeal. Let soak overnight to get them to "spit out" their sand and rinse thoroughly before cooking.

soups

white bean, spicy italian sausage and kale

Rich and robust, this unpretentious soup could easily be part of a satisfying dinner when served with a baguette from Au Soleil Levant and our Warm Pear, Walnut and Stilton salad on page 66.

serves 6

ingredients

1 lb dried white navy beans
4 oz chunk of bacon, diced
4 spicy italian sausages, uncooked
3 tbsp olive oil
2 cups onions, diced
2 cups carrot, grated
2 cups celery, chopped
5 garlic cloves, crushed
1 tbsp fresh thyme, chopped
1 tsp fresh rosemary, chopped
½ tsp red chili flakes
½ tsp salt
1 tsp pepper
12 cups low sodium chicken stock
5 cups fresh kale, de-stemmed and chopped
¾ cup parmigiano reggianno, grated

method

Rinse the beans in a colander.
Place beans in a large, heat proof bowl and cover with eight cups boiling water.
Let soak for 1 hour.
Sauté diced bacon on medium heat for 5 minutes. Squeeze sausage meat out of the casing directly into the same pan, break up meat with a fork and sauté until cooked.
Place in colander and let the fat drain.
Heat olive oil to medium in a large, heavy-bottomed stockpot and sauté onions, carrots and celery until softened.
Add garlic and sauté for another 2 minutes.
Drain and rinse the beans in a colander and add to the stockpot.
Add the cooked sausage and bacon, thyme, rosemary, red chili flakes, salt and pepper and the stock.
Turn heat up to medium high and bring soup to a simmer.
Cover pot with a lid and cook for 30 minutes or until beans are just tender.
Add the kale and cook until just wilted, about 3 minutes.
Serve and garnish with parmigiano reggianno.

The addition of the fresh kale gives you the healthy leafy greens that we all need. Did you know that one cup of kale has more than your daily requirement of vitamin C?

rich marsala oxtail soup with mustard thyme cream

Although "oxtail" sounds a bit unusual, it renders a different and richer flavour than a regular beef soup bone. Finding and using oxtail bones is well worth the delicious result – you won't go back!

serves 6-8

ingredients

2 lbs oxtail pieces*
2 tbsp tomato paste
2 medium carrots, chopped coarsely
2 stalks celery, chopped coarsely
1 large onion, diced
4 garlic cloves, whole and unpeeled
2 tbsp olive oil
1 tsp salt
1 tsp pepper
1 1/4 cups marsala wine
8 cups beef stock
1 package (1/2 oz) dried porcini mushrooms
2 bay leaves
2 sprigs fresh thyme
1/2 cup parsley, chopped for garnish

*available at the Railway Station Speciality Meats and Deli.

mustard thyme cream
1/2 cup sour cream
1 tbsp grainy dijon mustard
2 tsp fresh thyme, chopped
1/2 tsp salt
1/2 tsp pepper

method

Preheat oven to 400°.

Cover oxtail pieces with tomato paste and place them in a large roasting pan with carrots, celery, onion and garlic.

Drizzle everything with olive oil and sprinkle with salt and pepper.

Mix gently and roast for 45-50 minutes until browned, stirring occasionally, uncovered, during roasting time.

Remove garlic from roasting pan, transfer all other ingredients to a large, heavy bottomed soup pot, squeeze garlic from skins and add to soup pot.

Add marsala to the roasting pan that you were using for the vegetables. To deglaze pan, bring to a boil, stirring browned bits from bottom of pan for 2-3 minutes.

Pour reduced marsala and bits from the roasting pan into the soup pot.

Add beef stock, porcini mushrooms, bay leaves and thyme.

Bring stock mixture to a boil, reduce to low heat, cover and simmer gently for 2 1/2 - 3 hours until oxtail is very tender.

Remove oxtail and let cool.

Strain remaining ingredients through a colander over a large bowl. The stock will be caught in the bowl and you can return it to the soup pot.

Remove bay leaves and thyme sprigs from vegetable mixture.

Purée vegetable mixture and one cup of the strained stock, using a hand-held mixing wand or food processor and return to soup pot.

Remove all meat from the oxtail pieces and chop it finely, discarding any fat.

Return the meat to the soup pot (give the bones to the dog!).

Simmer over medium heat for another 20 minutes to combine flavours.

Whisk together sour cream, dijon, thyme, salt and pepper.

Garnish soup with a spoonful of mustard thyme cream and fresh thyme sprigs or parsley.

This is one of those all day soup making events, so pick a rainy, yucky day, turn on CBC radio and cozy into your kitchen!

nathan's malaysian coconut & seafood soup

Canadian culinary celebrity, Nathan Fong, is an old high school friend and has shared this fantastic noodle soup recipe with us. Nathan says "this is probably one of my absolutely favourite noodle dishes because it has every taste sensation you can think of…and it can be a hearty meal all by itself!" Thanks Nathan!

serves 6

ingredients

laksa paste - makes 1 ½ cups
4 serrano chilis, seeded
4 shallots, peeled
1 tbsp fresh ginger, peeled and coarsely chopped
1 tbsp fresh galangal root*, peeled and coarsely chopped
3 cloves garlic, peeled
2 stalks lemongrass, tender white part only
10 blanched almonds
2 tbsp coriander seed
1 tsp ground cumin
3 tbsp tamarind paste*
2 tbsp vegetable oil
¾ cup water

*available at Ellison's Market.

8 cups low sodium chicken stock
2 chicken breasts, skinless and boneless
8 ozs rice noodles (half of a 1 lb package)
1 ½ cups laksa paste
¾ lb firm white fish (snapper or halibut), cut into 1 inch pieces
12 large prawns, thawed, peeled and deveined, tails off
12 small scallops, thawed
2 tsp brown sugar
1 ½ tsp salt
2 cans coconut milk
6 tbsp green onions, sliced for garnish
6 tbsp fresh mint or cilantro, chopped for garnish

method

Place all laksa paste ingredients (except water) in food processor and blend for one minute.
Add water and process for another 2 minutes, until smooth.
Transfer mixture to a small saucepan and cook at a simmer for 40 minutes, stirring quite often until sauce browns slightly.
Remove from heat and allow to cool.

Bring stock to a boil in a large stockpot.
Add whole chicken breasts and simmer for 15 minutes.
Remove and cool slightly, then thinly slice or shred chicken breasts and set aside.
Place rice noodles in a large bowl and cover in boiling water for 5 minutes or until al dente, while chicken is poaching.
Drain and rinse noodles in cold water and set aside.
Bring stock back to a boil, add laksa paste and simmer for 5 minutes.
Increase heat to high, add fish, prawns and scallops and cook for 3 minutes.
Remove seafood with a slotted spoon and set aside.
Add sugar, salt, coconut milk and shredded chicken to the broth and cook for 10 minutes over medium heat.
Pour a ladle full of the hot soup over the cooked seafood and let sit for 2-3 minutes to reheat.
Place noodles in colander and pour boiling water over them to reheat, when you are ready to serve.
Divide into six soup bowls.
Divide seafood into the six soup bowls on top of the noodles then ladle hot soup with chicken over the noodles and seafood, garnish and serve.

The laksa paste is really what makes this soup so delicious. You can buy it ready made in Asian supermarkets, but why not make your own? No MSG! Make a double batch and freeze it in small ziplocs or keep it in the fridge for up to a week.

chipotle yam and corn chowder

Marianne's father taught her about the magical restorative powers of a good soup. His motto was "to avoid crisis, serve soup". Many a frozen skier or hungry child has been revived back to good humour with this delicious and nurturing chowder. No trace of dairy either, despite its creaminess.

serves 6

ingredients

5 medium yams, peeled and cubed
12 cups vegetable stock
2 tbsp olive oil
1 onion, finely chopped
3 cloves garlic, crushed
1 tbsp canned chipotle peppers, finely
  chopped
1/2 cup red pepper, finely chopped
1 cup frozen corn kernels, thawed
1 tsp adobo sauce (sauce chipotles are
  canned in)
1 lime, juice and zest of
salt to taste

method

Place cubed yams in a large stockpot and cover with eight cups of vegetable stock.
Boil for 30 minutes or until yams are completely tender.
Heat oil in sauce pan, sauté onion, garlic, chipotle and red peppers until tender, and set aside.
Remove 1 cup of cooked yams from the stockpot and set aside.
Purée yams and cooking water in the stockpot with hand-held mixing wand, or food processor, until smooth.
Add remaining four cups of stock to the puréed yams in the stockpot.
Add corn, adobo sauce and sautéed onion mixture.
Add juice and zest of lime.
Return reserved cup of cooked yams back into the stockpot.
Heat until just boiling, adjust salt and serve.

Because we rarely use a whole can of chipotle peppers in one recipe, we purée the leftover chipotles and freeze them in a small container. Then, when you need a spoonful for another recipe, just dig it right out of the container in its frozen state!

really green split pea soup

The innovative film caterer, Jane, pulled another trick out from under her apron strings one cool but spring-like day at work. She made the usual green split pea soup but then stirred in a lot of fresh puréed peas right at the end, adding a deliciously fresh and beautiful touch of spring to a hearty winter soup. It's sooo good!

serves 8

ingredients

2 tbsp olive oil
1 large carrot, peeled and diced
1 stalk celery, peeled and diced
1 medium onion, diced
1 tsp dried thyme leaves
2 bay leaves
4 cups vegetable stock
1 ½ cups dried green split peas
1 ham bone (optional)
2 cups frozen peas, thawed

method

Heat oil in a large stockpot.
Sauté carrot, celery and onion over medium heat until they are softened.
Add thyme and bay leaves and sauté for 2 minutes.
Add vegetable stock, dried peas and ham bone and stir well for 1 minute.
Reduce heat to medium low and allow soup to simmer for 1 ½ hours, stirring occasionally. Soup is done when the peas have completely fallen apart.
Remove ham bone (if using).
Purée thawed peas in a food processor or in a blender with a bit of water until they are still slightly chunky.
Stir pea purée into soup, increase heat to medium high and heat for 10 minutes, stirring frequently. To retain the beautiful colour of the soup, do not overcook the soup at this point.
Serve immediately with thick slices of fresh toasted sourdough bread from the Kaslo Sourdough Bakery.

Spit pea soup is traditionally made with a ham bone left over from a big ham dinner. If you don't have one, you can use a drop or two of liquid smoke to add that smoky flavour to the soup, if you like. It is available at most grocery stores. We used to be able to find smoked split peas now and again in our days on the movie catering truck. Grab some if you happen upon them, they are incredible! Of course, leaving the ham bone out is a good vegetarian option and the soup still tastes amazing!

sopa de black bean with salsa crema

Everyone (except Mike Adams!) craves a bowl of hearty black bean soup once in a while, especially when accompanied by a chunk of cornbread spread with jalapeño jelly. Recipes for these two sides can both be found in the first Whitewater Cooks, Pure, Simple and Real.

serves 8-10

ingredients

2 cups dried black beans
2 tbsp vegetable oil
2 medium onions, diced
1 jalapeño pepper, seeded and finely diced
3 cloves garlic, crushed
1 red pepper, diced
1 tsp cumin
1 tsp coriander
1 tsp oregano
1 tsp canned chipotle peppers, chopped
8 cups low sodium chicken or vegetable stock
1-28 oz can diced tomatoes with juice
½ cup Runaway Train barbeque sauce* (or any good quality barbeque sauce)
2 tbsp fresh lime juice
1 cup cilantro, chopped
salt and pepper to taste

salsa crema
½ cup sour cream or plain yogurt
2 tbsp store bought salsa

method

Combine the beans with enough water to cover by 3 inches and soak for at least 4 hours or overnight.
Sauté the onions in oil over medium heat in a large stockpot until soft.
Add jalapeño pepper, garlic, red pepper, cumin, coriander, oregano and chipotle peppers and sauté 5 minutes.
Drain the beans and add to the stockpot.
Add chicken or vegetable stock, canned tomatoes and barbeque sauce.
Cover partially and simmer over medium heat until the beans are tender, about 2 hours.
Purée with a hand-held mixing wand or a food processor until desired consistency is reached.
Add lime juice, cilantro, salt and pepper to taste.

Combine sour cream and salsa in a bowl.

Serve by topping each bowl of soup with a spoonful of salsa crema.

*Runaway Train barbeque sauce is our absolute favourite. One of the secret ingredients is Oso Negro coffee, which gives it a subtle kick! It is available at Ellison's Market and Culinary Conspiracy.

gazpacho in a glass with dungeness crab and avocado salsa

On a hot August afternoon, with your feet cooling in the lake and your hands around a glass of this cold, fresh tomato soup, spiked with crab and avocado salsa, and topped with a crispy crostini, beach potlucks will be taken to a whole new level.

serves 8-10

ingredients

4 cups tomato juice (or 2 cups clamato and
  2 cups tomato juice)
7 fresh ripe tomatoes, diced
2 cups vegetable stock
2 tbsp olive oil
2 tbsp red wine vinegar
3 cloves garlic, crushed
2 long english cucumbers, seeded and
  diced finely
1/3 cup red onion, diced finely
1/3 cup fresh basil, chopped
1/3 cup parsley, chopped
2 red peppers, diced
1/2 cup sherry
salt and pepper to taste

crostini
1 baguette
1/2 cup olive oil
3 garlic cloves, halved

salsa
1 cup dungeness crabmeat, coarsely
  chopped
2 avocados, diced
2 tbsp cilantro, chopped
1 lime, juice of

method

Combine tomato juice, tomatoes, stock, olive oil, red wine vinegar and garlic in a large bowl and whisk until well blended.
Add cucumbers, onion, basil, parsley, red pepper and sherry.
Purée with a hand-held mixing wand or in a food processor, until still slightly chunky.
Season with salt and pepper to taste.
Cover and refrigerate overnight.

Cut baguette into 1/2 inch slices and brush with olive oil.
Bake at 350° until golden brown and remove from oven. Rub each baguette slice with halved garlic clove.

Combine crab, avocado, cilantro and lime juice and toss gently, just before serving.

Place a spoonful of the crab salsa into the bottom of individual clear glasses or soup bowls.
Ladle gazpacho into each one and top with a crostini.

Drizzle with sour cream or plain yogurt if desired.

For a pretty presentation, put a spoonful of the crab salsa on top of the crostini as well as in the bottom of the glass.

paella chowder

Studded with spicy sausage, prawns and saffron-hued rice, this intriguing soup will remind you of the traditional flavours of paella and Spain. Hearty and flavourful, this is a perfect year-round soup.

serves 4-6

ingredients

2 tbsp olive oil
1 medium onion, diced
1 carrot, diced
2 stalks celery, diced
1 tsp lobster paste (optional)
¼ cup long grain white rice
½ tsp saffron threads, crushed
1 cup white wine or dry sherry
4 cups low sodium chicken stock
½ cup whipping cream
2 smoked italian sausages, sautéed and cut
  into thin diagonal slices*
1 cup frozen peas, thawed
1 chicken breast, cooked and sliced
¾ lb uncooked prawns, shelled and
  deveined
2 tbsp green onions, chopped

*available in the meat section at Safeway.

method

Heat oil in heavy-bottomed stock pot over medium heat.
Add onion, carrot and celery and sauté until soft, about 3-4 minutes.
Stir in lobster paste, if using.
Add rice, saffron, wine (or sherry) and stock and bring to a simmer.
Cover and let simmer until vegetables and rice are soft, about 20 minutes.
Remove from heat and cool for 10 minutes.
Purée everything (including the rice) with a hand-held mixing wand or in a food processor, then stir in the whipping cream.
Return the soup to low heat and add sausage, peas and chicken.
Heat for 10 minutes on medium heat.
Add prawns and cook until they are pink, about 3 minutes.
Garnish with green onions and serve.

Puréeing the rice in this interesting soup leaves it with a smooth and rich texture.

tana's tomato and red lentil bisque

Tana is probably the most vivacious person you could ever meet and her flavourful personality shines through in this soup...she loves it so much that she says she could bathe in it!

serves 8-10

ingredients

2 tsp cumin seeds, toasted
1 tbsp olive oil
1 medium onion, diced
2 garlic cloves, crushed
1 tsp fresh ginger, minced
1 tsp mustard seeds
1 green jalapeño, seeded and finely diced
1 tsp turmeric
1 tsp coriander
1/2 tsp cinnamon
2 bay leaves
2 cans (14 oz) diced tomatoes, or 3 cups fresh, diced
8 cups vegetable or chicken stock
2 tbsp tomato paste
1 cup red lentils, rinsed
2 cans coconut milk
sea salt and freshly ground pepper to taste
1 lime, juice of
1/2 cup cilantro, chopped for garnish

method

Toast cumin seeds in dry frying pan for a few minutes until they are aromatic, about 1 minute.
Grind them with a mortar and pestle or in a clean coffee grinder.
Heat oil in large soup pot, add onion, garlic, ginger, mustard seeds and jalapeño and sauté for 3-5 minutes.
Add ground cumin seeds, turmeric, coriander, cinnamon and bay leaves and sauté for 3-5 minutes.
Add tomatoes, stock, tomato paste and red lentils and let simmer for about an hour.
Add the coconut milk and simmer for 20 minutes.
Remove bay leaves and season with salt and pepper to taste.
Stir in fresh lime juice and garnish with chopped cilantro.

If you are in a hurry, serve this soup with a piece of na'an bread or a quesadilla for a quick, hearty meal.

the soup meister's wild mushroom & barbequed chicken soup

Soup Meister, Ralf Dauns, has a wildly successful soup bistro at the Lonsdale Quay in North Vancouver. This rich and hearty bowl of deliciousness definitely has some rib-sticking qualities.

serves 8-10

ingredients

2 tbsp vegetable oil
1 cup red onion, finely diced
4 garlic cloves, minced
2 packages dried wild porcini mushrooms
1 cup yellow fleshed potatoes, peeled, and diced
1 cup yams, peeled and diced
2 tbsp balsamic vinegar
1 cup white wine
1 lemon, juice of
4 cups low sodium chicken stock
1 cup whipping cream
1 cup demi-glace (or good beef stock)
½ cup good quality barbeque sauce
2 tbsp sweet chili sauce
2 tsp adobo sauce (the sauce from canned chipotle peppers)
3 cups mushrooms, sliced and sautéed
2 cups barbequed chicken, thinly sliced or shredded

method

Heat oil in a large, heavy bottomed stock pot over medium heat and add onions and garlic.
Saute for 2-3 minutes, until translucent.
Add dried porcini, potatoes and yams and sauté for 2 more minutes.
Add balsamic vinegar, white wine and lemon juice and let simmer for 2 more minutes.
Add chicken stock, whipping cream, demi-glace (or beef stock), sweet chili sauce, barbeque sauce and adobo sauce and simmer for about 20 more minutes.
Purée all ingredients with hand-held mixing wand or food processor until smooth.
Add sautéed mushrooms and shredded chicken and heat soup thoroughly.
Serve immediately, drizzled with a little truffle oil, like the Soup Meister does, if you like.

If you don't have any barbequed chicken handy, you can substitute a roasted chicken from your local grocery store.

salads

orchid lime salad

Way back when Nelson's original Rice Bowl was still open, we couldn't get enough of this salad. Toddlers at our feet, it would be one of our Kootenay moms' outings after a hike. This is our version of the original bowl of goodness!

serves 8

ingredients

dressing
$1/2$ cup peanut butter, smooth
1 lime, juice and zest of
2 tsp sesame oil
4 tbsp sweet chili sauce
4 tbsp rice vinegar
4 tbsp tamari or soy sauce
1 tbsp maple syrup
4 cloves garlic, crushed
2 tbsp fresh ginger, peeled and grated
$1/2$ bunch cilantro, chopped
$1/4$ cup vegetable oil

salad
one 16 oz package pad thai rice noodles
1 kettle full of boiling water
2 tbsp sesame oil
2 carrots, julienned
$1/2$ long english cucumber, seeded and julienned
1 red pepper, julienned
2 cups bean sprouts
1 bunch green onions, sliced diagonally
2 tbsp butter
1 cup slivered almonds
3 tbsp sesame seeds, toasted
$1/4$ tsp chinese five spice
1 tsp salt
1 tsp sugar

method

Blend all dressing ingredients except cilantro and oil with a hand-held mixing wand or in a food processor until just mixed.
Add oil in a steady stream while mixing until incorporated.
Stir in half of the cilantro and set aside.

Place rice noodles in a large bowl, cover with boiling water and soak for 10 minutes or until just tender.
Drain into colander, rinse with cold water, place back in to bowl and toss with sesame oil.
Add julienned carrots, cucumbers, red pepper, bean sprouts and green onions to noodles and set aside.
Heat butter in heavy-bottomed pan, add slivered almonds, sesame seeds, chinese five spice and salt and toss until golden brown, about 3-4 minutes.
Add sugar and toss for another 30 seconds.
Remove from heat and allow to cool thoroughly.
Add dressing to noodles and mix gently together with your hands or two wooden spoons.
Garnish with remaining cilantro, the toasted sesame seeds and almonds.

Unless you are going to eat all the salad in one sitting, don't dress all the noodles. Keep them separate and dress as needed.

lizzie's kids broccoli salad

Kids love this salad and it's a great way to get them to eat their veggies. Test driven on many a Kootenay kid!

serves 6-8

ingredients

dressing
½ cup plain yogurt
¼ cup mayonnaise
2 tsp sugar
½ lemon, juice of
½ tsp dill
½ tsp salt
½ tsp pepper

salad
3 cups broccoli florets, blanched and drained
½ cup red onion, diced finely
¼ cup sunflower seeds, toasted
½ cup dried cranberries
½ cup feta, crumbled

method

Combine yogurt, mayonnaise, sugar, lemon juice, dill, salt and pepper in a small bowl and whisk well.

Place broccoli, onion, sunflower seeds, cranberries and feta in a large bowl.

Pour dressing over the broccoli mixture 1 hour before serving and toss well.

To blanche broccoli or any vegetables, dip them in boiling water in a large pot for 1-2 minutes, until their colour is brilliant. Drain and immediately plunge into a sink full of cold water. Remove when cool and drain well. Store wrapped in paper towel in a plastic bag in the fridge until ready to use.

thai steak and soba noodle salad

Although this chef is not officially a "friend" who shared this recipe, we wish he was, because he is hot!...and a haute chef!
This salad was discovered and devoured in his chic bistro in Montreal and has become one of our favourites.

serves 4-6

ingredients

marinade
1/3 cup soy sauce
1/3 cup tomato paste
4 tbsp ginger, peeled and minced
4 tbsp garlic, crushed
2 tbsp honey
1 tsp sesame oil
1 tbsp sambal oelek (ground chili paste)
1 bay leaf
1 1/2 lb flank or sirloin steak

drizzle
1/4 cup rice vinegar
1 tbsp hoisin sauce
1/4 cup sweet chili sauce
1/2 tsp sesame oil

dressing
1/4 cup peanut butter, smooth
1/4 cup rice vinegar
1/2 cup good quality mayonnaise
1 tsp sambal oelek
3 tbsp hot water
2 tbsp fresh lime juice

salad
6 cups mixed seasonal greens
2 cups soba noodles*, cooked, cooled and tossed in a tablespoon of olive oil
2 carrots, julienned
1 cup sugar snap peas, halved
4 tbsp unsalted peanuts, toasted and chopped

*available at the Kootenay Co-op and Ellison's Market.

method

Combine all marinade ingredients and pour over steak in a glass or ceramic dish.
Cover and refrigerate for at least 4 hours, or overnight.

Mix peanut butter, rice vinegar, mayonnaise, sambal oelek, hot water and lime juice together and blend until smooth with a hand-held mixing wand or food processor.

Whisk together rice vinegar, hoisin, sweet chili sauce and sesame oil well, to make drizzle, then place in squeeze bottle.

Grill the steak for about 5 minutes per side (for medium rare), let rest for 5 minutes on a cutting board and slice diagonally in thin strips.

Toss the greens with some of the dressing and mound on individual salad plates.
Place a quarter of the soba noodles on top of the greens.
Assemble steak slices on soba noodles, top with carrots, sugar snap peas and chopped peanuts.
Finish with a squeeze of the drizzle sauce.

With the leftover dressing, you can create another delicious vegetarian salad by using our Sesame Tofu Coins on a bed of greens (recipe found on page 36), instead of the steak.

warm pear, stilton and walnut salad with orange marmalade dressing

This beautiful salad of golden roasted pears on a bed of baby romaine, sprinkled with stilton and walnuts proves that fruit, cheese and nuts were made for each other.

serves 6

ingredients

salad
1 tbsp balsamic vinegar
1 tbsp olive oil
4 medium anjou pears (not too ripe)
8 cups baby romaine or mixed baby greens
1/2 cup walnut pieces, toasted
1/2 cup stilton or blue cheese, crumbled

dressing
2 tbsp red wine vinegar
1 tbsp orange marmalade
1 tbsp fresh orange juice
1 tsp dijon mustard
1/2 tsp salt
1/2 tsp pepper
1/4 cup olive oil

method

Preheat oven to 400°.
Whisk together vinegar and oil in a small bowl.
Halve the pears lengthwise and core.
Place pears in shallow roasting pan and brush on all sides with the vinegar and oil mixture.
Roast pears, cut side up, for 10 minutes, then turn them over and roast for 10 more minutes, cut side down, until tender.
Cover pears with foil to keep warm while you assemble the salad.

Whisk together vinegar, marmalade, orange juice, dijon, salt and pepper.
Add oil in steady stream, whisking until incorporated.
Toss the romaine with 1/4 cup of the vinaigrette in a large bowl.
Place romaine on plates and set two pear halves on top, cut side up.
Sprinkle with walnuts and crumbled stilton and drizzle with remaining dressing.

If you know anyone with a walnut tree, grab some! Fresh walnuts are far superior to the store bought ones.

chickpea, quinoa and roasted yam salad

Make a big bowl of this hearty salad and keep it in the fridge. Then, when you get home from biking and you are starving, you can grab a wholesome and filling bowlful.

makes 4 cups

ingredients

dressing
3 tbsp white balsamic vinegar
1 tbsp dijon
1 tsp honey
2 cloves garlic, crushed
1/2 tsp pepper
1/2 cup olive oil

salad
1/2 cup quinoa
1 1/2 cups yams, peeled and cut into 1/2 inch cubes
1 tbsp olive oil
1/2 tsp pepper, cracked
1/2 tsp sea salt
two 14 oz cans chickpeas, rinsed and drained
1 carrot, peeled and grated
1 red pepper, diced
1/2 cup sunflower seeds, toasted
1 cup spinach, chopped coarsely
1/2 cup parsley, chopped
1/2 cup feta cheese, crumbled

method

Whisk together vinegar, dijon, honey, garlic, pepper and olive oil in small bowl and set aside.

Place quinoa and 3/4 cup cold water in a medium saucepan and bring to a boil. Immediately reduce to low heat and simmer for 15 minutes or until tender.
Turn heat off, leaving lid on, and let stand for 5 minutes.
Cool quinoa on a baking sheet.
Toss yams in olive oil, cracked pepper and salt and spread on a parchment lined baking sheet.
Roast in a 350° oven until just tender, about 20 minutes.
Place chickpeas, grated carrots, red pepper, sunflower seeds, spinach, parsley, feta, cooled quinoa and yams in a large bowl.
Pour dressing over all ingredients in bowl and toss gently until mixed well.

Adding leftover turkey or chicken to this turns it into the ultimate "fridge" salad.

retro spinach salad with maple soy dressing

Classic spinach salad – the way I remember it when my ahead-of-her-time and artistic mother Bernice made it back when I was in highschool. Bring it to a retro party!

serves 4

ingredients

salad
½ lb sliced bacon
½ cup green onions, sliced
6 cups spinach leaves, washed and dried
2 cups mushrooms, thinly sliced
1 cup sliced almonds, toasted
3 eggs, hard-boiled, peeled and crumbled

dressing
2 tbsp maple syrup
2 tbsp balsamic vinegar
1 tbsp soy sauce
1 clove garlic, crushed
1 tbsp sesame oil
1 tsp pepper
½ cup olive oil

method

Fry bacon in hot pan until very crispy.
Remove from heat and drain on paper towel. When cool, crumble or chop.
Reserve bacon fat and in medium hot sauté pan, fry green onions until crispy.
Remove and drain on paper towel.

Combine all dressing ingredients except oil and whisk well. Add oil in steady stream until incorporated.

Place spinach, crumbled bacon, crispy green onions, mushrooms, almonds and eggs in large salad bowl or on a serving platter.
Toss all the ingredients with dressing when ready to serve.

Wash spinach really, really well. It is often full of sand and may need multiple washings.

ancient grains and edamame with smoked paprika vinaigrette

Edamame, quinoa, wild rice, bulgur...all these things are so good for you! What could become dangerously close to becoming TOO healthy is instead a flavour sensation of exotic and fresh, thanks to the smoked paprika and fresh mint.

serves 6

ingredients

salad
1 $\frac{1}{2}$ cups frozen corn kernels, thawed
1 tbsp olive oil
$\frac{1}{2}$ tsp salt
$\frac{1}{2}$ tsp smoked paprika
$\frac{1}{2}$ cup wild rice
$\frac{1}{2}$ cup farro*
$\frac{1}{2}$ cup quinoa
1 $\frac{1}{2}$ cups frozen and shelled edamame
  beans, thawed
$\frac{1}{2}$ medium red onion, finely diced
2 tsp salt
1 cup fresh mint, coarsely chopped

*anicent european grain, available at the
Kootenay Co-op.

vinaigrette
$\frac{1}{2}$ tbsp fresh lemon juice
2 tbsp sherry vinegar
$\frac{3}{4}$ tsp smoked paprika
$\frac{1}{4}$ cup olive oil

method

Toss corn kernels in olive oil, salt and $\frac{1}{2}$ tsp of smoked paprika and roast in a 400° oven for 15 minutes or until golden.
Remove from oven and cool.
Place wild rice in medium saucepan and cover with 1 $\frac{1}{2}$ cups cold water.
Bring to a boil and immediately turn heat down to low.
Simmer at a low boil for 45-50 minutes until tender.
Drain and cool.
Cover farro with 2 cups of cold water in a sauce pot. Bring to a boil, immediately reduce to simmer and cook until tender, about 25 minutes, and drain and cool.
Place quinoa in medium saucepan and cover with $\frac{3}{4}$ cup cold water and bring to a boil, immediately reduce to simmer, and cook until tender, about 15 minutes.
Let sit for 5 minutes with lid on to steam, then cool.
Place all cooled grains in large bowl and add roasted corn, edamame, onion, salt and mint.

Whisk lemon juice, sherry vinegar, smoked paprika and olive oil together in a small bowl until blended.
Pour vinaigrette over grain mixture and toss very well.

To preserve the texture of the grains, cool them on cookie sheets.

sheri's salad nicoise

The multi-talented and beautiful Sheri made this as a dinner for us at her house in Maui and we loved the blending of the classic French and the lightness of the grilled fresh tuna. A beautiful loaf of olive bread with some herb butter and we were in heaven!

serves 6

ingredients

vinaigrette
¼ cup champagne vinegar
1 tsp fresh lemon juice
2 cloves garlic, minced
2 tbsp dijon
1 tbsp grainy dijon
1 tsp honey
½ tsp ground pepper
1 tsp fresh or dried tarragon
¾ cup extra virgin olive oil

salad
18 baby red or fingerling potatoes
1 lb fresh green beans, trimmed and
   blanched
2 tbsp mayonnaise
2 tsp honey
1 ½ lbs fresh ahi tuna steaks or albacore
   loins
½ tsp salt
½ tsp pepper
2 heads butter lettuce, gently washed and
   patted dry, left in whole leaves and set
   aside in fridge
2 cups grape or cherry tomatoes, halved
1 cup nicoise olives*
1 cup marinated artichoke hearts, quartered
3 eggs, hard-boiled, peeled and quartered
½ cup fresh parsley, chopped for garnish

*available at most delis (use kalamata
instead if you can't find nicoise)

method

Combine vinegar, lemon juice, garlic, dijon, grainy dijon, honey, pepper and tarragon in a small bowl and whisk well.
Add oil in steady stream until incorporated and set aside.

Put the potatoes and a pinch of salt in a large saucepan with enough cold water to cover them by one inch and bring to a boil.
Reduce to a simmer and cook until easily pierced with a skewer, about 15 minutes.
Drain and let cool slightly.

Preheat barbeque to medium heat.
Cut the potatoes in half, toss with ¼ cup of the dressing and set aside.
Combine the mayonnaise and honey in a small bowl.
Season the tuna steaks with salt and pepper and coat both sides with the mayonnaise mixture.
Grill the tuna for 1-2 minutes per side and transfer to a cutting board and slice into half inch thick strips.

Place the whole lettuce leaves on six individual serving plates.
Arrange potatoes, green beans, tomatoes, olives, artichoke hearts, eggs and sliced tuna on top of the lettuce.
Drizzle with the tarragon vinaigrette and garnish with chopped parsley.
Serve immediately.

In France, salad nicoise is made with tarragon. But, if you prefer fresh basil, you can substitute the tarragon in the dressing with 2 tbsp of chopped basil and add some leaves to the lettuce layer.

japanese spinach gomae

Traditionally, Gomae is a little cold spinach salad that is such a nice way to start a sushi dinner. It is also a great bright side dish for pairing with our Sesame Crusted Ahi Tuna recipe on page 98.

serves 6

ingredients

2 lbs fresh spinach, washed
½ tsp salt
1 ½ tsp sugar
1 tsp dried tuna flakes, crumbled (bonito tuna flakes)*
6 tbsp sesame seeds, toasted
½ tsp sesame oil
3 tbsp soy sauce
1 tbsp rice vinegar
2 tbsp water

*Packages of bonito flakes come in 30g sizes and are available at the Kootenay Co-op and Evergreen Natural Foods and Fruit Stand.

method

Bring a large pot of water to a boil.
Add salt and drop spinach into boiling water for 1 minute only.
Remove from boiling water, immediately drain in colander and run under cold water to stop cooking process and let drain.
Squeeze the excess water out of the spinach very well, using your hands or a wooden spoon.

Place sugar, bonito flakes, and two thirds (4 tbsp) of sesame seeds in food processor and blend together until just coarse but blended.
Add sesame oil, soy sauce, rice vinegar and water and blend until incorporated.
Remove and place in medium bowl.

Place squeezed spinach in bowl with dressing and toss until well coated.

Roll the dressed spinach into logs and cut each log into 2 inch lengths or serve in a little pile on a small platter.
Top by sprinkling with remaining sesame seeds.

Adding bonito flakes to your favourite miso soup recipe can use up the remaining flakes you will have left over.

roasted beets, goat cheese and pumpkin seeds on spicy greens

Beets are inexpensive, good for you, beautiful and delicious. Roasting the beets retains all their flavour, makes peeling them really easy and you won't end up with pink fingers! This is a great lunch salad or side dish for anything off the barbeque.

serves 6

ingredients

salad
6 medium size or 12 baby beets
8 cups spicy salad greens*
1 cup pumpkin seeds, toasted
4 oz goat cheese, crumbled

*spicy greens, which often include arugula, mustard greens and mizuna are available at Kootenay Co-op.

vinaigrette
¼ cup red wine vinegar
¼ cup honey
1 tbsp dijon
2 tbsp fresh dill, chopped
1 tsp salt
½ tsp pepper
¾ cup olive oil

method

Rinse the beets well and pat dry.
Wrap them in tin foil and seal all edges, making a package.
Roast in a 350° oven, until soft when pierced with a fork, about 1 hour.
Remove from oven, cool, slice off each end of the beet off and peel with a paring knife.
Slice into rounds and set aside.
Assemble salad greens on a large platter or on individual plates.
Arrange sliced beets on top of greens.
Top with toasted pumpkin seeds and crumbled goat cheese.

Combine vinegar, honey, dijon, dill, salt and pepper in small mixing bowl and mix well.
Whisk in the olive oil, in a steady stream, until thick and incorporated.
Drizzle vinaigrette over layered salad.

In early summer when the baby beets have tender green tops and asparagus is in abundance, you can add both those ingredients to this salad.

crispy panko tofu on baby spinach leaves with glory bowl dressing

We weren't going to repeat any recipes from the previous Whitewater cookbooks, but this is actually a combination of two separate recipes from each book. This has become a favourite salad that we eat all the time and we didn't want you to miss out on this great combo!

serves 4

ingredients

glory bowl dressing
1/2 cup nutritional yeast flakes
1/3 cup water
1/3 cup soy sauce
1/3 cup apple cider vinegar
2 garlic cloves, crushed
2 tbsp tahini
1 1/2 cups vegetable oil

salad
1 package firm tofu, cut into 1 inch cubes
2 tbsp soy sauce
2 tsp sesame oil
1 tbsp rice vinegar
1 tbsp sweet chili sauce

2 tbsp corn starch
2 tbsp water

1 cup panko crumbs
4 tbsp vegetable oil (for frying)
6 cups baby spinach leaves
4 tbsp sesame seeds, toasted

method

Combine yeast flakes, water, soy sauce, vinegar, garlic and tahini in a blender or mix with a hand-held mixing wand and process until smooth.
Add oil in a steady stream and blend until incorporated.
Store in a glass jar or a plastic squeeze bottle in the fridge.

Place the tofu in a glass baking dish.
Mix together soy sauce, sesame oil, rice vinegar, sweet chili sauce and pour over tofu.
Cover with plastic film and marinate for an hour or longer in the fridge, turning the tofu over a few times.
Mix the cornstarch and water together in a small bowl.
Place the panko crumbs on a plate.
Remove the tofu from the marinade and dip each piece into the cornstarch mixture and then the panko, pressing firmly so the crumbs stick well.
Heat a sauté pan to medium and add oil.
Place the tofu pieces in the hot oil and sauté for about 2 minutes on each side or until golden brown.
Place spinach on a serving platter or individual plates, top with crispy tofu right out of the pan.
Sprinkle with toasted sesame seeds and drizzle with dressing.

A completely satisfying, meat-free, protein-filled lunch salad that will keep you going until dinner.

chopped salad with chicken, feta and grapes

The sheer crunchiness of this flavour-filled salad appeals to everyone, especially your teenagers. Use a clear glass bowl if you have one, layering the ingredients and drizzling with the dressing at the last minute.

serves 4-6

ingredients

salad
1 head romaine, coarsely chopped
1 basket cherry tomatoes, halved
1 small long english cucumber, seeded and diced
1 large avocado, diced
1 cup corn kernels, thawed
1/2 red onion, finely diced
1 cup grilled chicken breast, sliced thinly
1 cup red or green grapes, halved
1/2 cup feta cheese, crumbled
1/2 cup slivered almonds, toasted

dressing
2 tbsp mango chutney
1 tsp celery seeds
1 tbsp fresh mint, chopped
1 tbsp honey
1 tsp dijon
2 tbsp sherry vinegar
1 tsp salt
1/2 tsp pepper
1/2 cup olive oil

method

Layer lettuce, tomatoes, cucumber, avocado, corn, red onion, chicken, grapes, feta and almonds in a clear glass bowl.

Whisk together chutney, celery seeds, mint, honey, dijon, sherry vinegar, salt and pepper in a small bowl.
Add oil in a slow, steady stream until incorporated.
Drizzle over chopped salad and toss to coat well with dressing.

This yummy concoction is also delicious wrapped in a pita or made into a satisfying sandwich with a fresh crusty baguette.

susi's jewelled salad

"Find a big beautiful platter with a little depth, something that makes your heart sing; turquoise always looks amazing with this salad!" This is how our dear friend Susi describes one of her favourite recipes...and as DH Lawerence said, "The human soul needs actual beauty more than food."

serves 8-10

ingredients

salad
1 head green or red lettuce, washed, spun dry and torn
3-4 large leaves of purple kale, washed, ribs removed, and finely chopped
1-2 cups arugula , or mizuna when available
1/4 -1/2 red onion, finely sliced
1 yellow or red or purple pepper, finely sliced
1 medium to large red or striped beet, raw, grated and sliced (for garnish)
1 medium golden beet, raw, grated
3 mini cucumbers, finely sliced
6-10 radishes, (if available use purple, white, magenta etc.) finely sliced
1 pomegranate, seeds only*

1/2 cup fresh mint leaves, finely chopped
1/2 - 1 tsp sumac**
1/3 cup sliced almonds, toasted

**a middle eastern spice with a very lemony flavour, available at Culinary Conspiracy.

dressing
1/3 cup olive oil
1 lemon, juice of
3 tsp Braggs (gluten-free soy sauce)
3 tsp honey
1/2 cup fresh mint leaves, finely chopped
1/2 tsp sumac
freshly ground pepper to taste

method

Make a bed of the torn lettuce leaves.
Scatter it with the finely chopped kale and the arugula or mizuna leaves.
Sprinkle with the red onion.
Layer cucumbers, radishes, pepper slices, chopped fresh mint and the sliced almonds.
Place the grated beets in small piles, alternating the two colours around the edge of the salad.
Sprinkle the middle of the salad with 1/2 tsp of the sumac spice.

Combine all dressing ingredients and mix well.
Drizzle the dressing over the composed salad and toss gently just before serving.

Pomegranate seeds really make this the "jewelled" salad, but using other fruit is equally stunning and delicious. If pomegranates are not available, you can use 1 cup seedless watermelon, diced and chilled, or 1 cup fresh red currants, raspberries, blueberries, blackberries, sliced fresh figs, or a combination of all of the above. Be creative!

tuscan bread salad with the best basil vinaigrette ever

My creative and wonderful stepmother Marcia shared this recipe with us from her cozy little home in Qualicum Beach. Bread salad is a nice change from greens and grains and the basil vinaigrette is so great, you will use it on everything!

serves 6-8

ingredients

basil vinaigrette
2 garlic cloves, crushed
1 $\frac{1}{2}$ tbsp dijon mustard
2 tbsp honey
$\frac{1}{4}$ cup red wine vinegar
1 tbsp balsamic vinegar
2 cups fresh basil leaves
$\frac{1}{2}$ tsp salt
1 $\frac{1}{2}$ tsp pepper
1 cup olive oil

salad
6 cups day old bread, crusts removed, cut into
  bite size pieces
2 red peppers, roasted* and sliced into wide
  strips
2 yellow peppers, roasted* and sliced into wide
  strips
3 medium tomatoes, cut into wedges
$\frac{1}{3}$ cup capers, rinsed
4 anchovy fillets, roughly chopped or whole
  (optional - only if you like them!)
$\frac{1}{2}$ red onion, sliced into thin rings
2 cups fresh mozzarella bocconcini balls,
  medium size (4x50g) quartered

$\frac{1}{2}$ cup fresh basil leaves, for garnish

method

Combine all vinaigrette ingredients, except olive oil and blend in food processor or blender.
Add oil in a slow steady stream until incorporated.

Place the bread pieces in a large salad bowl and toss with a $\frac{1}{2}$ cup of the vinaigrette.
Let sit for 20 minutes.
Add the peppers, tomatoes, capers, anchovies (if using), red onion and fresh mozzarella, and toss gently.
Drizzle with more vinaigrette until everything is coated well.
Toss and serve garnished with basil leaves.

To roast peppers, place them whole on a hot barbeque, lid down, and roast until skins are black and blistered. Cool in a paper bag. Slip skins off peppers while running under cold water. Slice open and remove seeds and stems.

entrees

blake's panko crusted miso sablefish

Zen fish master, Blake, used to be a commercial fisherman and knows his fish like no one else. His marinade is perfect for most fish, but really rocks this sablefish. Add a panko crust and voila – fish perfection!

serves 6

ingredients

six 6 oz pieces, 2 ¼ lbs fresh sablefish (also known as black cod)
1 tbsp miso paste
2 tbsp grainy dijon mustard
2 tbsp dijon mustard
½ cup low sodium soy sauce
2 tbsp wasabi paste (from tube)
¼ cup olive oil
½ fresh lemon, juice of
3 tbsp fresh ginger, peeled and finely grated
2 tsp garlic, crushed
2 cups panko bread crumbs
3 tbsp cornmeal
¼ tsp salt
¼ tsp pepper
3 tbsp olive oil

method

Whisk together miso, grainy dijon, regular dijon, soy sauce, wasabi paste, olive oil, lemon juice, ginger and garlic until well mixed.

Pour over fish pieces in a shallow pan, making sure all sides are coated and cover pan with plastic film.

Marinate for 45 minutes in the fridge.

Combine panko, cornmeal, salt and pepper and place on a large plate.

Remove fish from marinade and place on another plate.

Heat olive oil in heavy bottom pan on medium heat, until a crumb of crust mixture sizzles when you drop it in.

Dip fish pieces in panko mix and coat on both sides.

Sauté fish in pan until the panko crust is golden brown, about 4 minutes per side and serve immediately.

You could also leave off the panko crust and grill this fish on the barbeque or bake in a 400° oven for 15 minutes.

Test your fish for perfect doneness by flaking it gently with a fork. If it effortlessly separates and appears slightly shiny and opaque in the very middle, it is done!

michele's chicken charmoula

My very adored and admired friend Michele Repine and I shared an apartment in Paris while attending cooking school. We have kept our mutual devotion to food alive, both as a love and a career.

serves 8

ingredients

charmoula
2 tbsp cumin seeds
4 garlic cloves, crushed
2 cups cilantro, coarsely chopped
1 cup italian parsley, chopped
1 tbsp paprika
1/4 tsp cayenne pepper
1 tsp salt
1 1/4 cups olive oil
1 lemon, juice of
1 tbsp rice vinegar

cucumber yogurt sauce
1/2 long english cucumber, grated and drained
1/2 lemon, juice of
1/4 cup fresh mint, chopped
1 1/2 cups plain yogurt (whole milk, not non-fat)
1/2 tsp sugar
1 tsp salt

chipotle harissa
one 220g can chipotle peppers in adobo sauce
4 tbsp honey
1 tsp rice vinegar

8-10 bamboo skewers, soaked in water
16-20 boneless, skinless chicken thighs
1 large lemon, halved and quartered
1 red onion, cut into wedges

method

Toast cumin seeds in a small sauté pan over moderate heat, until fragrant, about 1-2 minutes.
Grind seeds to a powder, in a cleaned coffee grinder or a Magic Bullet food grinder.
Place ground cumin seeds, garlic, cilantro, parsley, paprika, cayenne, salt, olive oil, lemon juice and rice vinegar in a food processor and blend until mixture is just combined, about 30 seconds.
Set aside.

Stir together the drained cucumber, lemon juice, mint, yogurt, sugar and salt and set aside.

Place the can of the chipotle peppers, honey and rice vinegar in a food processor and purée until smooth.

Thread 2 whole chicken thighs, 1 lemon quarter and 1 red onion wedge onto each skewer.
Place in a shallow, glass or ceramic dish and pour on 3/4 cup of the charmoula sauce, coating the chicken well.
Marinate for a minimum of 2 hours or overnight.
Grill the skewers on a preheated, medium/hot barbeque for 4-5 minutes per side or until juices run clear.
Serve with bowls of the remaining charmoula sauce, the cooling cucumber yogurt sauce and the chipotle harissa sauce arranged around the platter of chicken skewers.

Put a teaspoon of each sauce on your plate and savour the flavourful elements of the completely indivdual tastes. Using a firm white fish or lamb on the skewers,will produce equally enticing results in this unforgettable dish.

roasted chinese five spice and garlic chicken

The simple pleasure of eating roast chicken is heightened when using this intriguing marinade. Combining this succulent chicken with the Orchid Lime salad, on page 60, is a great way of smugly having a flavourful dinner ready in no time.

serves 4-6

ingredients

1 whole organic chicken, about 3 lbs
8 garlic cloves, crushed
2 tbsp salt
4 tbsp sesame oil
¼ cup vegetable oil
2 tsp chinese five spice powder
4 tbsp rice vinegar
1 cup cilantro, chopped
1 tsp red chili flakes
2 limes, quartered, for garnish

method

Place the chicken, breast side down, on a cutting board so the back is facing you. Using a sharp knife or kitchen scissors, cut through the ribs on one side of the backbone.

Lay chicken open, cut through the ribs on the other side of the backbone and remove the backbone completely.

Discard the backbone.

Flip chicken over and crack the breastbone by pressing down on the flat side of a knife laid across the breast, until chicken lays flat.

Combine garlic, salt, sesame oil, vegetable oil, chinese five spice, rice vinegar, cilantro and chili flakes in large bowl.

Place chicken in marinade and flip around a few times to coat it on all sides.

Cover with plastic film and marinate in fridge for at least 4 hours or overnight.

Preheat oven to 350°.

Remove chicken from marinade, place in a roasting pan and roast in oven for about 1 to 1 ½ hours or until juices run clear when a skewer is poked into the thigh joint.

Cut chicken into pieces, place on serving platter and garnish with lime wedges.

Why should you learn how to split a chicken? Well,because once you've oven roasted or barbequed a whole split chicken, you'll never go back! The dark and white meat cook evenly and perfectly.

gussy's ribs

These are the best baby back ribs shared by the amazing caterer and great pal Annie Bailey. She used to make them at a local restaurant called "Gussy's". One of her biggest fans was the owner, a cute man named Gus Adams, who has remained very special to Annie for 34 years. These are for him!

serves 8-12

ingredients

4-6 racks of baby back ribs, thawed

broth
10 cups hot water
1 tbsp dried whole rosemary
1 tsp dried thyme
1 tsp dried oregano
1 cup powdered beef stock or demi-glace
1 tsp garlic salt
1 tsp pepper
6 bay leaves

barbeque sauce
$1/4$ cup vegetable oil
$1/2$ cup red onion, diced
10 cloves garlic
1 canned chipotle pepper, diced
$1/2$ tsp black pepper
$1/4$ tsp salt
2 cups good quality barbeque sauce
$1/2$ cup maple syrup
$1/2$ cup brown sugar
$1/3$ cup jack daniel's bourbon
1 orange, juice and zest of

method

Place ribs in deep roasting pan.
Combine hot water, rosemary, thyme, oregano, beef broth, garlic salt, pepper and bay leaves.
Pour broth over ribs and cover with tin foil or a tightly fitting lid.
Roast in a 350° oven for 2-2 $1/2$ hours. Check ribs after 1 $1/2$ hours because some ribs are smaller and won't take as long. Meat should be very tender.
Remove ribs from broth and let them cool on parchment lined baking sheets.

Sauté onion in vegetable oil until just soft in a heavy bottomed medium sized pot.
Add garlic, chipotle pepper, salt, barbeque sauce, maple syrup, brown sugar, jack daniels and orange juice and zest.
Let simmer on low heat for 15 minutes, stirring often.

Baste ribs with generous amounts of the barbeque sauce on both sides.
Roast in a 350° oven for 40-45 minutes.

These delicious ribs could also be cooked on the barbeque on low heat. Have several finger bowls around because they are messy!

pat's tuesday night pasta sauce

Growing up with an Italian mother and a trio of sisters, Pat could have stayed right out of the kitchen. Thankfully for all of us lucky pals, he obviously didn't! We all dream about driving down our driveways, and finding a husband like Pat hovering over the stove, creating traditional pasta dishes with mucho amore!

serves 10

ingredients

one 2 lb package penne rigate
1/4 cup extra virgin olive oil
3-4 hot italian sausages, uncooked
  and 3-4 mild italian sausages, uncooked
1/2 cup fresh basil, chopped
2 tbsp dried oregano
1 bunch green onions, chopped
1 medium onion, diced
1 red pepper, diced into 1/2 inch squares
1 green pepper, diced into 1/2 inch squares
1 cup mushrooms, sliced
3 bay leaves
2 chicken bouillon cubes
1 jar (650 ml) good quality tomato sauce
2 cans (398 ml) diced tomatoes
1 1/2 cups half and half cream
1 cup parmesan, grated
1/2 cup parmesan, grated, for the table

method

Heat oil in a deep frying pan on medium high heat.

Squeeze sausage meat from the casing directly into the pan and break uncooked sausage up into little pieces with a fork.

Add basil and oregano and sauté with sausage about 8-10 minutes, until done.

Add green and white onions, red and green peppers, mushrooms, bay leaves and chicken bouillon cubes and cook for another 10 minutes, being careful not to overcook the vegetables.

Add tomato sauce and diced tomatoes and then bring to a low boil for 30 minutes.

Add half and half cream and 1/2 the parmesan and let simmer for 20 minutes.

Boil penne in salted water until al dente and drain.

Toss penne with about 2 cups of the sauce (just enough to coat it) and place on a serving platter.

Top pasta with another 2 cups of sauce and the remaining parmesan.

Place remaining sauce in serving bowls and set around the table along with the parmesan.

Buying good quality pasta sauce, pasta and homemade sausages is totally worth it. Go to Star Grocery in Trail, B.C. and ask for Pasquale!

monica's cedar plank salmon

Among her many talents, my stepsister Monica is a phenomenal cook. Whether she is in her own gorgeous kitchen or in the galley of her boat in Desolation Sound, every dish she flings together is always delicious and beautiful. Here is her version of cedar plank salmon, worthy of our own B.C. best!

serves 6

ingredients

one 1 ½-2 lb salmon fillet
one cedar plank, long enough to fit the salmon, soaked in water for at least 4 hours

topping

3 tbsp capers, very roughly chopped
1 cup fresh parsley, chopped
½ cup fresh basil, chopped
¼ cup fresh dill, chopped
¼ cup fresh thyme, chopped
1 tsp dried oregano
¼ cup fresh chives, chopped
2 shallots, diced
2 garlic cloves, crushed
¼ cup olive oil
¼ cup butter, melted
2 lemons, juice and zest of

sauce

¾ cup sour cream
1 tbsp fresh dill, chopped
1 tbsp capers

lemon wedges
1 bunch green onions

method

Preheat barbeque on high, then reduce heat to medium/low.
Combine all topping ingredients in medium bowl and mix well.

Lay salmon on plank, skin side down and cover with topping.
Place plank on barbeque and cook for 20-25 minutes, lid down. Salmon is done when the natural fat of the salmon has risen to the surface of the filet.
Serve the salmon right off the plank.

Mix sour cream with chopped fresh dill and capers together in a small bowl to serve with salmon.
Surround the salmon with lemon wedges and grilled green onions.

To have a supply of planks for your summertime barbequing, you can buy a whole plank of untreated (1x8 inch) cedar siding at your local lumberyard and have them cut it into your 16 inch lengths. You can also buy singles at most kitchenware or big grocery stores.

pulled pork enchiladas with mole sauce

The flavour and texture delivered by this dish is well worth the effort. You can make the pork and the mole sauce the day before, then assemble the enchiladas when you are ready to make dinner. Feel free to double the recipe to maximize your efforts. You can easily freeze the extra pork in a Ziploc bag and the mole sauce in a plastic container. Next time you have a hankering for these enchiladas, it will be really easy!

serves 6

ingredients

one 2 $\frac{1}{2}$ lb pork butt
4 cloves garlic, crushed
2 tsp cumin
2 tsp oregano
1 tsp salt
1 tsp pepper
2 tsp liquid smoke
1 medium onion, diced
2 cans (12 oz) whole tomatillos, drained
 and puréed with a hand-held mixing wand
1 cup low sodium chicken stock
6 (9 inch) corn or flour tortillas
1 cup chicken stock, heated
2 cups manchego or mozzarella cheese, grated

mole sauce

2 tbsp vegetable oil
1 medium onion, diced
4 cloves garlic, crushed
2 tomatoes, diced
4 tbsp pumpkin seeds, toasted
3 tsp brown sugar
1 tsp canned chipotle pepper, chopped finely
2 tsp oregano
1 tsp cinnamon
2 cups low sodium chicken stock
4 tbsp cider vinegar
3 oz bittersweet or Mexican chocolate, grated
1 tsp salt
1 tsp pepper

method

Preheat oven to 350°.
Place the pork butt in a roasting pan and sprinkle with garlic, cumin, oregano, salt, pepper and liquid smoke.
Add onion, tomatillos and chicken stock, cover with tin foil and roast in oven for 2 hours.
Remove tin foil and roast for another $\frac{1}{2}$ hour until tender.
Transfer pork roast to a platter and allow to cool slightly, reserving the tomatillo mixture.
Shred the pork along the grain of the meat by hand and place in medium bowl.
Add $\frac{1}{2}$ the tomatillo mixture to the pulled pork and reserve the other half. Set aside.

Heat oil and sauté onion, garlic and tomato for 2 minutes.
Add the pumpkin seeds, brown sugar, chipotle pepper, oregano, cinnamon, chicken stock, vinegar and chocolate, and simmer uncovered for about 20 minutes.
Purée with a hand-held mixing wand or in a food processor until smooth and add salt and pepper.
Cover the bottom of a greased baking dish with the reserved tomatillo sauce.
Dip a tortilla in the heated chicken stock and lay on a working surface.
Place $\frac{1}{6}$ of the pulled pork on the tortilla, roll up and lay seam side down on top of the tomatillo sauce; repeat procedure for remaining tortillas.
Coat the enchiladas with the mole sauce, top with the grated cheese, then cover with tin foil and bake for 30 minutes.
Remove tin foil and return to oven for 10 minutes to brown the cheese.

sesame crusted tuna with ginger sake cream

When we needed a decadent entree to make our guests swoon, we tried pairing fresh tuna with a creamy and flavourful sauce. And swoon they did...so will yours! We like to serve this tuna dish with a rice noodle stir fry or perfectly cooked basmati rice.

serves 6

ingredients

¼ cup vegetable oil
½ cup fresh ginger, peeled and thinly sliced
½ medium onion, finely chopped
2 garlic cloves, thinly sliced
2 tbsp rice vinegar
¼ cup fresh lime juice
4 tbsp sake
1 tsp sriracha chili sauce*
1 tsp honey
1 ½ cups whipping cream
1 tsp salt
½ tsp pepper

six 6 oz tuna steaks
½ cup sesame seeds, toasted

*available at Wing's grocery.

method

Heat 2 tbsp of the oil in a saucepan.
Add the ginger, onion and garlic and sauté for about 5 minutes, until soft.
Add the vinegar, lime juice, sake, chili sauce and honey and simmer until the liquid has almost evaporated, for about 10 minutes.
Add the whipping cream and simmer until reduced by half, about 30 minutes.
Strain sauce through a strainer over a pot.
Season with salt and pepper and keep warm.

Place the sesame seeds on a plate and press both sides of tuna into the seeds firmly.
Heat remaining oil in sauté pan to medium high heat.
Add the tuna and sear, turning once, cooking it 2 minutes per side; sesame seeds should be browned and tuna rare.
Slice the tuna into half inch slices or serve in a whole piece, drizzled with the ginger sake cream.

To make perfect basmati rice, this is what we do:

Heat a tablespoon of oil in a heavy-bottomed medium saucepan for 2 minutes. Add ½ cup uncooked rice per person and stir in oil until the rice looks translucent, about 3-4 minutes. Add 1 ½ times cold water to rice, bring to a boil with lid on and immediately turn to low and allow to simmer, lid on, until fluffy and done. White basmati will be done in 15 minutes and brown will take 30 minutes. Turn heat off and let sit on stovetop with lid on for another 5 minutes to "steam" it to perfection!

cashew lamb riblets with saffron curry sauce

There are so many fabulous Indian restaurants in Vancouver and this recipe is a marriage of many great dining experiences we have had while spending time in this stunning city.

serves 6

ingredients

3 racks of lamb, trimmed and cut into chops (about 18-20)
¼ cup vegetable oil
1 tbsp cumin
1 tsp salt
½ tsp cayenne pepper
1 tbsp coriander
1 tsp paprika
½ tsp turmeric
1 tbsp garlic, crushed
1 cup cashews, unsalted, toasted and pulsed in a food processor until coarse

saffron curry sauce (makes 3 cups)
½ tsp saffron
¼ cup very hot water
3 tbsp vegetable oil
1 tsp cumin seeds
½ tsp fenugreek seeds
4 kaffir lime leaves
1 tbsp garlic, crushed
½ tsp turmeric
1 tsp salt
½ tsp cayenne pepper
1 tsp paprika
1 ½ cups coconut milk (1 can)
1 cup whipping cream
1 cup low sodium chicken stock
1 tsp sugar
1 lemon, juice of
1 tbsp corn starch mixed with 1 tbsp water
½ cup cilantro, chopped

method

Combine oil, cumin, salt, cayenne, coriander, paprika, turmeric, garlic and half of the cashews in a medium bowl and mix until well combined.
Place lamb chops in a single layer in a shallow baking dish and cover with marinade, coating all sides well.
Cover and place in fridge for no more than 2-3 hours.

Place saffron threads in a small bowl, add hot water and soak for 30 minutes.
Heat oil on medium high heat in heavy bottomed medium saucepan for 45 seconds.
Add cumin seeds, fenugreek and lime leaves and allow them to sizzle for 30 seconds.
Immediately add the garlic and sauté for 1 minute.
Add turmeric, salt, cayenne and paprika and sauté for another minute.
Add coconut milk, whipping cream, chicken stock, sugar and saffron infused water, increase heat to high until just boiling.
Turn heat down to low and let sauce simmer for 20 minutes until slightly reduced.
Add lemon juice and cornstarch mixed with water and whisk into sauce until combined and thickened.
Stir in cilantro and set aside.

Preheat oven to 500° and move rack to highest position
Arrange lamb chops on a large baking sheet without overlapping them.
Bake for 4 minutes, remove from oven, close the oven door, and with tongs, turn chops over, sprinkle quickly with remaining ground cashews, return to oven and bake for another 4 minutes, until medium rare.
Serve chops on individual plates drizzled with the saffron curry sauce.

This versatile and mild curry sauce is also excellent with grilled fish, chicken, and steamed vegetables...

porcini and sea salt crusted beef tenderloin with port reduction

My stepsister Monica is the queen of feeding large groups of friends, with ease, tons of love and no stress. Beef tenderloins are best left large and whole, so making her divine entree really works for big, fancy dinner parties.

serves 12-14

ingredients

1 whole beef tenderloin (8-10 lbs)
two ¾ oz packages dried porcini mushrooms
½ cup fresh rosemary, chopped
¼ cup coarse sea salt
½ cup dried onion flakes
¼ cup whole black peppercorns
¼ cup mustard seeds
6 garlic cloves, whole

port reduction

½ cup butter
2 cups shallots, chopped finely
6 garlic cloves, crushed
1 cup celery, chopped finely
1 cup red wine vinegar
2 cups port or red wine
½ cup fresh thyme, chopped
½ cup fresh rosemary, chopped
 4 cups demi-glace*

*available at Railway Station Specialty Meats and Deli.

This beef is so flavourful and tender that if you don't have time to make the port reduction, you could just serve it with a mixture of sour cream, horseradish and ground pepper.

method

Combine dried mushrooms, rosemary, sea salt, dried onion flakes, peppercorns and mustard seeds in a clean coffee grinder or Magic Bullet food grinder and process until fine and powdery. You may have to do this in a few batches.

Add garlic cloves to the last batch and process until garlic is just incorporated.

Mix all the batches together, rub all over the tenderloin and let sit overnight in a glass baking dish, covered with plastic film.

Melt the butter in a large heavy bottomed stock pot over medium/low heat and sauté the shallots, garlic and celery until soft, about 10 minutes.

Add the vinegar and reduce until the shallots and celery mostly absorb it, about 15 minutes.

Add the port (or red wine), thyme and rosemary and reduce by half, about 30 minutes.

Remove from heat and strain through a sieve, return broth to saucepan, add demi-glace and simmer for 20 minutes.

Preheat oven to 425°.

Remove beef from glass dish and place into a roasting pan.

Roast beef in hot oven for 15 minutes, turn oven down to 350° and roast for 45 minutes. If you want to use the barbeque instead, sear the beef on all sides on medium high heat, then turn down to low and roast for another 35-40 minutes.

Check for preferred doneness using a meat thermometer.

Remove from oven and let "rest" for at least 20 minutes and up to 45 minutes, covered with foil before slicing.

Serve drizzled with warm port reduction.

barb's rich and creamy gorgonzola sauce

Barb is full of personality! This sauce recipe she shared with us is as rich as her character. She loves to drizzle it on beef carpaccio, but it can be served on any cut of meat or vegetable dish that may need a bit of spark.

makes 1 **½** cups

ingredients

1 tbsp butter
1 tbsp flour
1 cup whipping cream
¼ cup dry white wine
¼ cup low sodium chicken stock
1 tbsp worcestershire sauce
1 cup crumbled gorgonzola cheese
½ tsp black pepper, freshly ground

method

Melt butter in a small saucepan.
Whisk in flour and stir over low heat for about a minute.
Whisk in whipping cream, wine, chicken stock and worcestershire sauce.
Bring to a boil, then reduce heat to low right away.
Stir in gorgonzola cheese and black pepper.

Store in a glass jar in the fridge until needed.

If you want to serve this sauce with beef carpaccio, sear the beef on all sides in a hot pan. Wrap with plastic film and refrigerate until cold. Remove plastic film and slice the beef very thinly with a really sharp knife. Arrange beef on a platter and drizzle with the warm sauce.

Also tastes great with our Porcini and Sea Salt Crusted Beef Tenderloin on page 102.

moroccan lemon chicken tagine with couscous

Another great skier's dish because it can easily be made the day before, quickly reheated and enjoyed when you get off the slopes, having smugly taken that last, LAST run...

serves 5-6

ingredients

12 boneless, skinless chicken thighs
2 tsp salt
2 tsp pepper
¼ cup olive oil
2 medium onions, thinly sliced
4 cloves garlic, crushed
1 tsp turmeric
1 tsp cumin
1 tsp coriander
½ tsp dried chili flakes
2 cinnamon sticks
2 bay leaves
3 cups low sodium chicken stock
2 lemons, zest and juice of
1 can chickpeas, rinsed and drained
1 cup pitted green olives, manzanilla or
 picholine are preferred
½ cup fresh mint, chopped
2 lemons, quartered

saffron couscous
2 cups couscous
2 cups low sodium chicken stock
3 tbsp butter
½ tsp saffron threads
1 tsp salt
¼ cup olive oil

method

Season the chicken all over with salt and pepper.
Heat olive oil in large, heavy bottomed stockpot over medium high heat.
Brown the chicken well all over, about 3-5 minutes per side and set aside.
Turn heat down to medium, add onions and garlic and cook until soft, about 5 minutes.
Add turmeric, cumin, coriander, chili flakes, cinnamon sticks and bay leaves and sauté, stirring constantly, until spices are fragrant, about 1 minute.
Add the chicken stock, lemon zest and juice, cover and simmer over low heat for 20 minutes.
Return chicken to pot, add the chickpeas and olives and stir to combine.
Simmer, uncovered, stirring occasionally until sauce has reduced somewhat and chicken is done, about another 20 minutes.
Stir in fresh mint and lemon quarters just before serving.

Preheat oven to 350°.
Place the couscous in an oven proof baking dish.
Heat the chicken broth, butter and saffron until butter is melted and the broth is hot.
Pour the mixture over the couscous and stir well.
Cover with foil and bake for 10 minutes until liquid has been absorbed.
Remove from oven and let sit, covered, at room temperature for another 5 minutes.
Drizzle olive oil over the couscous.

Serve chicken tagine over couscous.
Garnish with whole sprigs of fresh mint and grilled lemon halves, if you like.

You can easily double this recipe if you end up with a few additional hungry skiers around your dinner table.

asian spiced braised short ribs

The braising of short ribs is such a satisfying process, as the work involved is short and the long cooking time frees you up to prepare the rest of your dinner.

serves 6

ingredients

rub
6 lbs beef short ribs*
1/2 tsp chinese five spice powder
3 garlic cloves, crushed
2 tbsp ginger, peeled and minced
3 tbsp vegetable oil
1 tsp salt
1 tsp pepper

sauce
1 medium onion, sliced
1 bunch green onions, sliced
4 garlic cloves, whole and flattened
2 tbsp ginger, peeled and sliced
1/2 tsp dried red chili flakes
2 tbsp brown sugar
5 whole star anise
2 tbsp black peppercorns
1 cinnamon stick
1 orange, juice and zest of
1 bunch cilantro, chopped
1/2 cup sake or rice vinegar
4 tbsp soy sauce
1 cup red wine
3 cups beef stock

green onions and orange zest (for garnish)

*available at Railway Specialty Meats and Deli.

method

Mix together chinese five spice, garlic, ginger and oil.
Season short ribs with salt and pepper, then rub this mixture all over the ribs and set aside.

Preheat oven to 350°.
Heat a large heavy bottomed oven proof pot to medium high heat.
Add ribs and brown on all sides. You will need to do this in a few batches.
Remove and set aside.

Add onion, green onions, garlic, ginger and chili flakes to the same dutch oven and sauté until onion is soft, about 2 minutes.
Add brown sugar, star anise, peppercorns, cinnamon stick, orange juice and zest, cilantro, sake, soy sauce, red wine and beef stock and bring to a boil.
Return the ribs to the pot and cover with a lid.
Place in oven and bake for 2 1/2 hours until ribs are very tender.
Remove ribs from oven proof pot, cover with foil and set aside.
Strain sauce through colander, return to dutch oven and on medium heat on stovetop, reduce to about 2 1/2 cups of liquid, about 20 minutes.
Return ribs to sauce and reheat to serve.
Garnish with julienned green onions and orange zest.

We like to serve these spiced shortribs with plain basmati rice and steamed Chinese greens, like bok choy or gai lan.

mike's famous stuffing

My husband Mike makes Thanksgiving and Christmas dinner and always receives many compliments over his yummy stuffing at this festive occasion. It is very much appreciated by everyone, except that he insists on leaving the cranberry sauce in its can shape on the table and that kills me! But, never criticize when someone else cooks the meal!

makes about 10-12 cups of stuffing

ingredients

2 tbsp vegetable oil
3 cups celery, chopped
2 cups onions, diced
1 pound pork sausage, broken into small chunks
2 tart apples, diced with skin on
1 cup hazelnuts, toasted, skinned and chopped roughly
1 cup dried cherries
6 cups stale bread cubes
1 tsp salt
1 tsp fresh thyme, chopped
1 tsp fresh sage, chopped
1 tsp pepper
1 cup port
1 cup chicken stock

Stuffing belongs in a turkey and every year someone phones us on Thanksgiving Day wondering about just how to cook one! So, we've included a turkey cooking tip (see right).

method

Heat oil in large sauté pan over low heat.
Sauté the celery and onions until soft, about 10 minutes.
Transfer the sautéed vegetables to a large mixing bowl.
Add the sausage to the pan and cook breaking up the sausage with a wooden spoon until it is cooked through and lightly browned, about 10 minutes.
Add the sausage to the mixing bowl.
Stir the apples, hazelnuts and cherries into the sausage mixture.
Add the bread cubes and toss lightly.
Add the salt, thyme, sage, and pepper and toss again.
Add the port and chicken stock and stir to combine.
Stuff the turkey and place any remaining stuffing in an oven proof casserole dish covered with tin foil.

Rinse the turkey well and pat it dry. Stuff the cavity loosely with 7 cups of stuffing. Skewer the cavity shut. Stuff the neck area with another 3 cups of stuffing. Secure the neck skin flap under the turkey.
Place the turkey in a large enough roasting pan that ensures the sides don't touch the pan. Pour 3 cups of water into the pan.
Roast the turkey at 15 minutes per pound. Baste the turkey every hour with some melted butter. If the turkey skin starts getting too dark, make a foil tent and keep it covered.
You will know when it's done either by using a meat thermometer (to 165°) or visually checking by piercing the turkey deep in the inner thigh and watching for clear-running juice. If it is at all pink, return to oven.
Remove the turkey from the oven, keep it loosely covered and let it rest for at least 15 minutes before carving.
While the turkey is resting, strain the pan juices into a heavy-bottomed saucepan. Add enough stock and white wine to make 4 cups. Heat to a simmer.
Stir ¼ cup flour and ¼ cup water together until smooth. Whisk this into pan juices and heat to a boil. Reduce to a simmer and season with salt, pepper, 1 tsp sage, a dash of lemon juice and a splash of heavy cream. Serve hot gravy over warm turkey and stuffing!

pescado blanco fish tacos

Montana's best Mexican restaurant, Pescado Blanco, serves plates and plates of these fantastic fish tacos. David Lewis, owner and chef, has added his own innovative twist to an old Baja favourite and has kindly shared this delicious recipe with us. Thanks Dave!

serves 6

ingredients

chipotle crema
1 cup sour cream
4 tsp half and half cream
1 tsp adobo sauce (the sauce from the canned chipotle peppers)

orange avocado salsa
3 oranges, peeled, diced and drained
2 tbsp cilantro, chopped
2 tbsp jalapeño peppers, seeded and finely diced
2 tbsp red onion, diced finely
2 medium avocados, diced into 1/2 inch cubes
3/4 tsp salt

tacos
12 small corn tortillas
1 tbsp olive oil
1 1/2 lbs firm white grilling fish (red snapper, halibut or mahi mahi), cut into 1x3 inch strips
1 tsp chili salt* or make your own version by combining 1/2 tsp cumin, 1/2 tsp onion salt, 1/2 tsp paprika
2 cups red cabbage, very thinly shaved

*available at the Kootenay Co-op.

method

Whisk together sour cream, half and half cream and adobo sauce until well blended, then refrigerate.

Combine oranges, cilantro, chilis, red onion, avocado and salt, and mix gently with a spoon in a medium bowl.
Set aside.

Preheat oven to 300°.
Wrap tortillas in tin foil and place in oven for 15 minutes.
Sprinkle fish pieces with chili salt.
Heat oil in two sauté pans until almost smoking.
Divide fish into two batches and sear in individual hot pans until just done, about 3-4 minutes.
Lay two warm tortillas on each person's plate.
Spread a thin layer of red cabbage on each tortilla, followed by seared fish, then a spoonful of orange avocado salsa and finish with a dollop of chipotle crema.
Serve immediately.

When using fresh chilis, prepare them by slicing in half lengthwise, then removing the pith and seeds inside. This is the really hot part! We always test a tiny piece of the chopped chilis on our tongue, just in case they are way hotter than we thought. It is easier to add more chilis later, rather than try and tone down excess heat!

margie's pork tenderloin saltimbocca roasted on a bed of braised apples

A busy mother, coach, lawyer and dedicated friend, Margie excels at all of that and still manages to sit down everyday with her wonderful daughters to enjoy dinner hour. She shared this simple, beautiful and comforting recipe with us.

serves 4

ingredients

1 pork tenderloin (about 1 $\frac{1}{2}$ lbs)
2 tbsp dijon
1 tsp pepper
1 tsp salt
10 sage leaves (enough to cover top of pork)
4-6 prosciutto slices
4 pink lady or gala apples, sliced thinly, peels on
1 cup riesling (or gewürztraminer) wine
1 tbsp cold butter
2 tbsp maple syrup
1 tsp grainy dijon mustard

method

Brush dijon on top of pork.
Sprinkle with salt and pepper.
Place sage leaves all along the top of the pork.
Lay proscuitto slices on work surface one after the other, slightly overlapping in a row.
Place pork on prosciutto slices sage side down, wrap it around the pork and seal with your fingers.
Arrange apple slices in bottom of oven-proof roasting pan and drizzle with $\frac{1}{2}$ cup of the wine.
Put pork on top of apples with the sage side up.
Roast in preheated 375° oven for 30-35 minutes.
Remove from oven and set pork aside on a platter and cover with tin foil.
Place roasting pan on stove top at medium/low heat and add remaining $\frac{1}{2}$ cup riesling to apples to deglaze, about 2 minutes.
Add 1 tbsp cold butter, maple syrup and grainy mustard and simmer for 3 more minutes.
Slice the pork and serve it with the warm apples.

Braised red cabbage, mashed potatoes with caramelized onions and a green salad would complete this yummy dinner.

linguine with prawns, chilis and preserved black beans

This spicy, salty and very quick to make recipe is one we've been cooking for years. It's one of the first fusion type dishes that caught our eye.

serves 6

ingredients

3 tbsp olive oil
3 cloves garlic, crushed
1 medium onion, diced
½ tsp dried red chili flakes
4 tbsp chinese preserved black beans,
  soaked in hot water for 2-3 minutes and
  drained*
1 bag (454g) large prawns, raw and peeled,
  tails off (B.C. spot prawns are best)
2 large tomatoes, diced
1 lb linguine
2 cups arugula
freshly ground black pepper
fresh basil, chopped for garnish
1 cup grated romano cheese

*available at Wing's Grocery.

method

Bring a large pot of salted water to a boil for the linguine.
Heat the olive oil in a wok or large sauté pan, add garlic, onions and chili flakes and sauté over medium/low heat or until onions are soft.
Add preserved black beans and prawns and sauté for 2 minutes until prawns start to turn pink.
Add tomatoes, sauté for another 2 minutes until prawns are done and set aside.
Add linguine to the boiling water and cook until al dente.
Drain pasta, add to the sauce and combine well.
Reheat if necessary.
Toss in the arugula just before serving and stir gently.
Garnish with ground pepper and fresh basil and serve with romano cheese.

Once you've made this dish a few times, you'll figure out how hot you like it and adjust the chili pepper flake amount. It's also delicious made with scallops or chicken instead of prawns.

jane's beef bourguignon

Ever since the popular movie "Julie and Julia" featured the culinary influence of Julia Child, Beef Bourguignon has made a huge comeback. There are more ways than one to arrive at this most delicious of beef dishes and here is a recipe, with a twist, from the talented and highly entertaining movie chef, Jane.

serves 6

ingredients

one 6 oz chunk of bacon, cut into "lardons"
($\frac{1}{2}$ x $\frac{1}{2}$ inch cubes)
3 lbs stewing beef, cut into 2 inch cubes
3 tbsp flour
1 tsp salt
$\frac{1}{2}$ tsp pepper
1 carrot, peeled and sliced
3 cloves garlic, crushed
1 small jar (473 ml) pickled cocktail onions,
drained
3 cups red wine
3 cups beef stock
1 tbsp tomato paste
$\frac{1}{2}$ tsp fresh thyme, chopped
1 bay leaf
1 tbsp butter
1 pound mushrooms, quartered
$\frac{1}{2}$ cup parsley, chopped

method

Preheat oven to 325º.
Heat a heavy bottomed casserole pot to medium/high heat.
Add bacon and sauté for 4-5 minutes until bacon is crisp.
Remove the bacon, set aside and save bacon fat in pot.
Toss the beef cubes in a large bowl with the flour, salt and pepper until the beef is well coated.
Turn the heat up to high and add beef, in small batches, to the same pot with the bacon fat, sear on all sides until browned and set aside.
Place carrots, garlic and onions in casserole pot, turn heat down to medium, add a bit of oil if necessary and sauté vegetables until they are slightly browned.
Add wine, beef stock, tomato paste, thyme, bay leaf, sautéed beef and bacon lardons back into the casserole pot and stir gently to mix.
Heat to a simmer on top of the stove.
Cover the casserole and bake in oven for 4 hours, stirring a few times after 3 hours and returning to the oven with the lid off for the last hour.
Heat butter and sauté mushrooms at medium high heat for 4-5 minutes or until mushrooms are lightly browned. Set aside.
Remove beef from oven, add sautéed mushrooms and parsley to casserole pot and stir.

To make this dish ALL about awesome onion flavour, you can take the time to caramelize some onions and add them to the mashed potatoes that would be so great with this dinner. Beef Bourguignon only gets better as you let it sit, so you can easily make it the day before and reheat it slowly before serving.

halibut with macadamia nut crust and lobster saffron sauce

Decadent but doable! When you are spending as much of your hard earned money as you do on halibut, you may as well pull out all the stops and make this sauce, equal in quality and elegance.

serves 6

ingredients

2 tbsp butter
1 small onion, diced
1 cup fennel bulb, diced (save fronds for garnish)
1/2 tsp saffron threads, crushed
2 tsp lobster base* or 1 cup chopped lobster meat
2 tbsp tomato paste
1 cup white wine
1 cup fish stock or clam nectar
1 cup whipping cream
1 tbsp fresh squeezed orange juice

six 6 oz halibut filets
1/2 cup mayonnaise
1 cup macadamia nuts, unsalted
2 cups panko crumbs
1/2 tsp salt
1/2 tsp pepper

*available at Railway Specialty Meats and Deli.

method

Melt butter in a medium saucepan and sauté the onion and fennel until translucent.
Add saffron, lobster base (or chopped lobster meat), tomato paste, wine and fish stock and let simmer for about 20 minutes.
Add whipping cream and orange juice and let simmer for another 20 minutes until thickened.
Purée with a hand-held mixing wand until almost, but not completely smooth.

Preheat oven to 375º.
Place macadamia nuts, panko, salt and pepper in a food processor and pulse until mixture is the consistency of breadcrumbs.
Spread mayonnaise on the top of each filet and then coat with crumbs, pressing them in gently.
Bake in top third of oven for 15-20 minutes until fish is flaky and opaque and nuts are golden brown.
Serve on individual plates, sitting in a pool of lobster sauce.
Garnish with fennel fronds and a few strands of orange zest.

Making the effort to find lobster base is worth your time. Keep it in the freezer and spoon out a little bit as needed, as it really does add an amazingly rich taste to your seafood dishes.

desserts

peppi's biscotti tortoni

The memory of this favourite childhood dessert from Peppi's Restaurant in West Vancouver haunted Liz for years, until she managed to recreate the Italian delicacy. Thanks Liz!

serves 6

ingredients

2 cups whipping cream
$\frac{1}{2}$ cup half and half cream
$\frac{1}{2}$ cup icing sugar, sifted
1 tsp vanilla
1 cup one-bite coconut macaroons, crumbled and toasted
$\frac{3}{4}$ cup slivered almonds, toasted
$\frac{1}{3}$ cup marsala wine or sweet sherry
2 egg whites, beaten until stiff

method

Combine whipping cream and half and half cream with icing sugar and vanilla in a large bowl.

Beat until mixture forms soft peaks.

Freeze until firm, for 1 hour in the same bowl.

Preheat broiler.

Place crumbled macaroons on baking sheet and toast on middle rack of oven.

Toss macaroon pieces often while they are toasting, until they are golden on all sides.

Let cool and pulse in food processor until they resemble coarse breadcrumbs.

Place slivered almonds on baking sheet on middle rack of oven and toast until golden (watch closely, as it only takes 2-3 minutes!).

Cool and set aside.

Pulse the almonds in food processor until they are also the consistency of coarse breadcrumbs.

Combine almonds and macaroon crumbs in a large bowl, reserving $\frac{1}{4}$ cup for garnish.

Remove cream from freezer and stir in the macaroon mixture well.

Add marsala (or sherry) and mix again.

Fold in beaten egg whites gently until well blended.

Spoon mixture into a plastic film-lined loaf pan or mini muffin tins for individual servings, cover with plastic film and freeze until very firm.

Loosen biscotti tortoni from pan just before serving by wrapping a warm, wet cloth around the pan for a few minutes.

Invert onto a serving platter or individual plates.

Garnish with reserved macaroon almond mixture.

This dessert is delicious all on its own, but would also be great with chocolate sauce and raspberries.

vanilla bean crème brûlée

Marianne has been making this never fail, totally delicious vanilla crème brulee for years. If you've been too intimidated to make this elegant French dessert, here's the recipe that will change your mind.

makes 7 individual servings

ingredients

2 cups whipping cream
¼ cup 2% milk
1 vanilla bean
½ tsp vanilla
2 whole eggs, room temperature
4 egg yolks, room temperature
⅔ cup sugar
white sugar (for the crust)

method

Heat the whipping cream, milk, vanilla and vanilla bean to scalding or when the mix just begins to foam and expand, but not boil.

Set aside for 15 minutes and then remove the vanilla bean.

Beat together whole eggs, egg yolks and sugar until thick, creamy and pale, about 10 minutes.

Stir cream mix into egg mix, whisking constantly until incorporated.

Fill small ramekins (¾ cup size) to within ¼ inch from the top with mixture and place in a lasagna-type pan.

Add hot water to the pan and fill until water is halfway up the side of the ramekins (water bath).

Bake for 55 minutes in a 300° oven until set.

Remove pan from the oven, then the ramekins from water bath and let cool on a rack.

Sprinkle each ramekin with 1 tsp sugar when ready to serve.

Preheat broiler and set rack in the top part of the oven.

Place ramekins on a baking sheet under the broiler until sugar is melted and caramel coloured, about 3-5 minutes, depending on the strength of your broiler. Stay by the oven, keeping a constant eye on the crème brûlée, moving the pan around if you need to.

Serve at room temperature. To eat, crack the sugar crust and enjoy the creaminess underneath.

This is a great base recipe as you can infuse the milk with so many things to change the flavour. Orange or lemon zest, candied ginger bits, chai tea spices, lavender...they are all sublime.

If not serving right away, you can store them in the fridge overnight wrapped in plastic film and finish them in the oven.

classic coconut cake

Think "classic" and we think Petra! Beautiful, athletic and talented with sharp culinary skills to boot, it's no wonder this classic cake came from her. Thanks Petie!

makes one 9 inch layer cake

ingredients

coconut cake

2 cups flour
1 1/3 cups unsweetened flaked coconut, loosely packed
1 cup buttermilk
1 tsp baking soda
2 cups organic cane sugar
1 cup butter, room temperature
1/4 tsp salt
5 large egg yolks
4 large egg whites, room temperature, beaten until stiff peaks form

icing

one 8oz package regular cream cheese, room temperature
1/2 cup butter, room temperature
2 tsp vanilla
3 1/3 cups icing sugar
1 cup unsweetened flaked coconut, lightly toasted

method

Grease two 9 inch cake pans well.
Line bottom of pans with parchment paper rounds.
Mix flour and coconut in medium bowl.
Whisk buttermilk and baking soda in small bowl.
Beat sugar, butter and salt with beater in large bowl until light and fluffy, about 2 minutes.
Add egg yolks and beat until just blended, about 30 seconds.
Add 1/3 of beaten egg whites to batter and fold gently, with spatula, until just blended.
Repeat with other 2/3 of beaten egg whites.
Divide batter between 2 pans.
Bake at 350° for 35 minutes or until skewer inserted into middle comes out clean.
Cool cakes in pan for 10 minutes.
Run sharp knife around edge of pan and invert on to cooling racks.
Peel off parchment and cool cakes completely.

Combine cream cheese, butter and vanilla, and mix well in a food processor or with electric beaters.
Add icing sugar and beat again until smooth and spreadable.
Place first cake layer, flat side up, on a plate and spread with 1 cup of icing.
Place second layer, flat side up, on top of icing and spread remaining icing on the top and sides of cakes.
Sprinkle toasted coconut on top and sides of cake.

Serve at room temperature.

Room temperature ingredients make all the difference when cake baking. You can get more loft from non chilled egg whites, and room temperature butter is easier to cream with sugar than the straight from the fridge stuff. The fluffy egg whites and properly creamed butter and sugar produce a tender and light cake.

kootenay kids cupcakes

We wanted to have some sort of healthy version of the ever popular cupcake. We slipped in this hearty carrot cake recipe, cleverly disguised as a prettily iced little treat, so that kids and parents would be equally excited. You can still serve them at a kid's birthday with a candle...and a gummy bear!

makes 24 cupcakes

ingredients

cupcakes
1 ½ cups carrots, grated
¾ cup canned crushed pineapple, with liquid
¾ cup unsweetened coconut, toasted
¾ cup pecans, chopped
½ cup pitted dates, chopped
¾ cup brown sugar
⅓ cup white sugar
3 eggs, room temperature
2 tsp vanilla
¾ cup vegetable oil
1 ½ cups flour
1 tsp baking soda
2 tsp baking powder
½ tsp salt
1 ½ tsp cinnamon
½ tsp allspice
1 ½ tsp ground ginger
½ tsp ground nutmeg

cream cheese and white chocolate icing
8 oz (1 package) regular cream cheese, room temperature
¼ cup butter, room temperature
1 tsp vanilla
3 oz white chocolate, chopped
3 cups icing sugar, sifted
1 cup unsweetened coconut, toasted (for garnish)

method

Line muffin tins with cupcake liners.
Combine carrots, pineapple, coconut, pecans and dates in large bowl.
Mix the sugars with the eggs, add vanilla and then beat on high until volume has tripled.
Add oil slowly, on low mixing speed until blended.
Combine flour, baking soda, baking powder, salt, cinnamon, allspice, ginger and nutmeg in a bowl.
Add dry ingredients to the egg mixture and stir in gently.
Fold in carrot pineapple mixture.
Fill muffin tins to three quarters full.
Bake for 30 minutes at 350° or until a skewer comes out clean.

Beat cream cheese and butter on high until light and fluffy.
Stir in vanilla.
Melt white chocolate in a double boiler over medium heat and add warm chocolate to the cream cheese mixture.
Mix on high until smooth and fluffy.
Slowly add icing sugar, stopping to scrape down the sides of the bowl occasionally.
Ice the cupcakes when they are cool and top with lots of toasted coconut for garnish.

lava cakes with sour cherries and mascarpone cream

This fabulous dessert, reminiscent of Black Forest Cake, is one to pull out when you really want something decadent. You can prepare the lava cakes ahead of time, as they can live in the fridge, unbaked, for up to 24 hours. Just increase baking time to 20 minutes and enjoy! As a bonus, it's gluten-free for those who can't eat wheat.

serves 9

ingredients

mascarpone cream
1/2 cup whipping cream
1 tsp vanilla
2 tbsp light brown sugar
1 tsp lemon zest, finely grated
1 cup mascarpone cheese
1 tsp fresh lemon juice

1 cup canned sour cherries, drained
1/4 cup kirsch

lava cakes
9 small ramekins (3/4 cup size)
pan spray
9 small parchment paper circles, the size of
  the bottom of the ramekins
2 tbsp cocoa powder
1/2 cup butter
10 oz semisweet chocolate, finely chopped
1 1/2 cups sugar
3 tbsp cornstarch
3 whole eggs, room temperature
4 egg yolks, room temperature
2 tsp kirsch
1/4 cup icing sugar, sifted

method

Beat whipping cream, vanilla, brown sugar and lemon zest until soft peaks have formed.
Add mascarpone and lemon juice and mix until blended. Set aside in fridge.
Soak the sour cherries in the kirsch and set aside.

Spray ramekins well and lay parchment circle in the bottom of ramekin.
Sift cocoa through sieve into small bowl and dust greased ramekins on bottom and up sides with cocoa.
Melt butter and chocolate together in a double boiler. Cool slightly.
Mix sugar and cornstarch together in a large bowl.
Add melted chocolate and butter and combine well.
Whisk eggs, yolks and kirsch in a separate bowl until light, about 5 minutes.
Add egg mixture to chocolate mixture and combine well.
Spoon 1/2 cup of batter into each ramekin.
Bake at 400° until tops have set, and formed a cracked crust, about 15 minutes. Cakes will be gooey in the middle.
Cool for 2 minutes.
Run paring knife around edge of each cake and invert on to individual dessert plates.
Dust with icing sugar and serve with a dollop of mascarpone cream, finishing with a spoonful of kirsch soaked cherries and serve right away.

You could also serve these lava cakes in their ramekins and leave out the parchment circle liners.

hana banana bread

While travelling around even the most remote corners of Maui, we often came across small stands that sold freshly baked banana bread. Full of island delicacies like macadamia nuts, toasted coconut and ripe bananas, this treat inspired our version of "Hana Banana" bread.

makes 1 loaf

ingredients

1/4 lb butter, room temperature
1 cup brown sugar
2 large eggs, room temperature
1 1/2 cups white flour
1 tsp baking powder
1 tsp salt
1/2 cup shredded coconut, toasted
1 cup very ripe bananas, mashed
1/2 cup sour cream
1 tsp vanilla
1/2 cup unsalted macadamia nuts, chopped

method

Grease loaf pan.
Beat butter and sugar together in a large bowl until fluffy and light, about 5 minutes.
Add eggs, one at a time, until combined.
Whisk flour, baking powder, salt and toasted coconut together.
Add to butter mixture until just blended.
Add mashed bananas, sour cream and vanilla and mix until combined.
Stir in macadamia nuts.
Bake for 1 hour at 350° or until skewer comes out clean when inserted into the middle.
Let cool 10 minutes on rack and then invert out of pan. Cool completely before slicing.

If kids are involved, adding one cup of chocolate chips will make this bread even more appealing to them.

toffee crunch lunch box cookies

There's a certain trashy charm about these cookies in a white sugar, Skor bar kind of way. Although there is very little real health involved with these cookies, they are comforting and addictive! And if guilt takes over, eat extra broccoli at dinner tonight.

makes 2 dozen

ingredients

2 ¼ cups flour
1 tsp baking powder
½ tsp salt
½ lb butter, room temperature
¾ cup white sugar
¾ cup brown sugar
1 tsp vanilla
2 eggs
1 package (200g) Skor toffee bits
white sugar for sprinkling

method

Combine flour, baking powder and salt.
Beat together butter, sugars and vanilla until light and fluffy in a large bowl.
Add eggs and blend thoroughly.
Add flour mixture in thirds, mixing well after each addition.
Stir in toffee bits.
Drop by rounded teaspoon onto a parchment lined baking sheet.
Sprinkle with white sugar.
Bake in a 350° oven until golden brown, for about 12 minutes, switching cookie sheets around in oven halfway through baking.
Cool on rack when done.

Parchment paper is a worthy investment for baking. Cookies bake evenly, clean up is minimal and you can re-use it. Go buy some today!

rolled pavlova with lots of fresh fruit

Excited inspiration made us roll this pavlova instead of leaving it flat. This simple action melds the textures and flavours beautifully and the presentation is bound to garner some compliments too! Enjoyed by many at Baldface Cat Ski Lodge in the days when Emmy reigned there as pastry queen.

serves 6-8

ingredients

3 egg whites, room temperature
2 tbsp water
1 1/2 cups white sugar
1 1/2 tsp white vinegar
1 tsp vanilla
2 cups whipping cream
1/4 cup sugar
1 tsp vanilla
1/2 cup fresh strawberries, or any type of berries
1 fresh kiwi, peeled and sliced
1/2 cup red grapes, halved
1/2 cup canned or fresh peaches or mangoes, sliced
1 banana, sliced

1 cup fresh raspberries, puréed until smooth
1 cup fresh mangoes, puréed until smooth

method

Beat egg whites until stiff (make sure your beaters and bowl are thoroughly clean).
Add water and beat for another 2-3 minutes.
Add sugar, 1/2 cup at a time, beating well after each addition and scraping sides of bowl occasionally.
Add vinegar and vanilla and beat well until mixture is thick and shiny, about 5 minutes.
Spread mixture evenly onto parchment lined baking sheet to within one inch of the edge. Don't let mixture touch sides of sheet.
Bake for 20 minutes at 350° until light brown, with a firm crust.
Remove from oven and cool well at room temperature.
Line another baking sheet with parchment paper and hold it over the cooked meringue. In one smooth motion, invert the meringue on to the second baking sheet. Pull the inverted meringue, still on the parchment, on to a working surface.
Whip cream with 1/4 cup sugar and vanilla until firm.
Spread meringue with whipped cream and sliced fruit and roll up, beginning at the wide end of your rectangle. Crust will crack a bit.
Place on serving platter, seam side down.
Chill for a maximum of 1 hour.
Cut into one inch slices and serve on individual plates.
Serve with mango and raspberry coulis (puréed fruit) for a spectacular presentation!

You can freeze any leftovers and thaw ever so slightly just before serving! Reminds us of the Italian dessert, Semifredo.

emmy's pear and fresh ginger cake

Out of each of the previous Whitewater cookbooks, there emerged one cake recipe that became everyone's favourite go-to. We think this will be the one out of this book! Anything the beautiful and talented Emmy bakes is perfect, and this is another winner from her!

makes one 9 inch round cake

ingredients

3 cans (14 oz) pear halves, drained
2 tbsp brown sugar
¾ cup butter, room temperature
½ cup brown sugar
2 eggs, room temperature
½ cup molasses
½ cup honey
4 tbsp fresh ginger, peeled and grated finely
2 cups flour
2 tsp baking soda
½ tsp salt
1 cup sour cream

method

Wrap a sheet of tin foil around the bottom of a 9 inch springform pan so batter doesn't leak out while baking.
Grease the springform pan thoroughly and sprinkle the bottom with the 2 tbsp brown sugar.
Arrange pear halves round side up in the bottom of the pan in a circle, placing some in the middle as well. This part needs to look pretty so take your time!
Beat butter and sugar until light and fluffy, about 3-5 minutes.
Beat in eggs, one at a time, until just mixed in.
Add molasses, honey and ginger and mix until incorporated (mixture will look a bit curdled).
Sift flour, baking soda and salt together.
Fold one third of flour mixture into the batter, then a third of the sour cream and repeat until all ingredients are combined.
Gently spread the batter on top of the pears, taking care not to move the pears around.
Bake in a 350° oven for 1 hour 15 minutes, or until skewer inserted into middle comes out clean.
Cool for 20 minutes on rack and then flip cake over on to a serving platter, removing the sides and bottom of the springform pan.
Serve while still a bit warm or at room temperature with softly whipped cream.

You can use canned peaches instead of the pears. Yum.

barbie's buttery shortbread

Our best friends growing up were Tana and Cathy. Their mom Barb had many great recipes and this is one that Cathy immortalized on the catering truck. From there it ended up in all of our kitchens, always made with love and fond memories of the Tocher gals.

makes 40 small rectangles

ingredients

3 cups all purpose flour
1/2 cup cornstarch
1 cup icing sugar, sifted
1 lb butter, room temperature

method

Work all ingredients together, with your hands, until thoroughly mixed.
Form into a ball and knead 8 to 10 times on a lightly floured surface.
Press into a parchment lined 12x18 inch baking sheet.
Cut into 40 rectangles with a sharp paring knife.
Prick each piece twice with a fork.
Bake at 300° for 40 minutes until slightly golden.
Remove from oven, re-cut the scored rectangles to separate and let cool in the pan.

This dough also makes great cookie cutter shortbread. Roll dough out to 1/2 inch thick and cut out with cutters. Bake at 300° for 20 minutes. Let cool and decorate! Storing these in an airtight container ensures they will stay fresh for a few weeks – if they last that long!

lisa p's orange sour cream bundt cake

Gregarious and legendary movie catering chef Lisa P, makes countless great desserts. This is one of her most loved.

makes 1 bundt cake

ingredients

1 cup butter, room temperature
1 cup sugar
3 eggs, room temperature
1 cup sour cream
1 orange, zest of
1 ¾ cup flour
1 tsp baking powder
1 tsp baking soda
½ tsp salt

glaze
2 oranges, juice of
¾ cup sugar
1 lemon, zest of

method

Beat together butter and sugar until light and fluffy.
Add eggs, one at a time, beating well after each addition.
Add sour cream and orange zest and combine.
Sift together flour, baking powder, baking soda and salt.
Add dry ingredients to the creamed butter and beat until well mixed.
Spoon into well-greased bundt pan and bake at 350° for 40 minutes.

Combine orange juice, sugar and lemon zest in small saucepan.
Heat to a low boil, allow liquid to reduce by one third, about 10 minutes and keep warm.
Remove cake from oven and let cool for 10 minutes.
Invert cake onto serving plate.
Poke lots of holes into cake with a skewer and pour glaze over cake while both are still warm.

This also makes a great birthday cake. Substitute the glaze with our cream cheese icing, found in the Kootenay Kids Cupcakes recipe on page 122 and light the candles!

mini vanilla and baby mocha cheesecakes

While everyone loves cheesecake, it's hard to slice enough whole cakes elegantly for a crowd. Here's the solution! The divine blend of flavours and textures in these individual cuties delivers the essence of cheesecake. The marvelous Kim Irving came up with the mini vanilla ones and the baby mocha ones are a Whitewater Cooks recipe. Presented together on raised cake platters, this dessert is an easy undertaking with a sweet presentation.

ingredients

mini vanilla cheesecakes (makes 24)
1 package vanilla wafers
1 cup sugar
three 250g packages regular cream cheese,
   room temperature
4 eggs, room temperature
2 tbsp fresh lemon juice
1 tsp vanilla
2 cups whipped cream, for garnish
fresh fruit slices for garnish: kiwis,
   strawberries, raspberries, blueberries...

baby mocha cheesecakes (makes 12)
½ cup chocolate cookie crumbs
½ cup ground almonds
2 tbsp sugar
3 tbsp butter, melted
½ tsp cinnamon

1-250g package regular cream cheese, room
   temperature
¼ cup sugar
2 tbsp sour cream
1 egg, room temperature
2 oz good quality dark chocolate, melted
1 tsp espresso coffee, very finely ground
2 tbsp coffee liqueur or 1 tbsp vanilla
¼ tsp salt
1 cup whipped cream mixed with 1 tbsp
   sifted cocoa powder, for garnish
12 chocolate covered espresso beans, for
   garnish

method

mini vanilla cheesecakes
Line muffin tins with cupcake liners.
Place one vanilla wafer in each, flat side down.
Beat together sugar, cream cheese and eggs until smooth and creamy.
Add lemon juice and vanilla and mix until combined.
Spoon cream cheese mixture into muffin tins until three quarters full.
Bake in a 350° oven for 18-20 minutes.
Let cool and peel cupcake liners off.
Garnish with a dollop of whipped cream and seasonal fresh fruit.

baby mocha cheesecakes
Line muffin tins with cupcake liners.
Mix cookie crumbs, nuts, sugar, melted butter and cinnamon together.
Divide mixture evenly into the 12 cups and press firmly into the bottoms and set aside.
Place cream cheese and sugar in a food processor and blend until smooth and creamy.
Add the sour cream, egg, melted chocolate, ground espresso, coffee liqueur (or vanilla) and salt.
Mix well to combine.
Using a jug, pour the mixture into the 12 cups.
Bake in a 325° oven for 15 minutes. The cheesecakes will puff up a little in the oven and fall when you cool them.
Cool until set, about 30 minutes and peel cupcake liners off.
Garnish with cocoa whipped cream and a chocolate covered espresso bean.

Both little minis can be made the day before you need them. Garnish just before serving.

pauline's cranberry crumble bars

A treasured recipe from Pauline Riley, passed on to her dear friend Sue Lamb and now shared with us. It holds the contrast between sweet and sour that cranberry lovers everywhere will go wild for.

makes 16 bars

ingredients

base
¾ cup butter, room temperature
½ cup sugar
½ tsp vanilla
½ tsp cinnamon
1 ½ cups flour
½ cup ground almonds

filling
½ cup water
½ cup orange juice, fresh
1 cup sugar
2 tsp orange zest
3 cups fresh or frozen cranberries

topping
¼ cup flour
2 tbsp brown sugar
¼ tsp cinnamon
½ cup almonds, roughly chopped
2 tbsp cold butter

method

Place butter, sugar, vanilla, cinnamon, flour and ground almonds into large bowl and mix with your hands or a pastry blender until combined.
Press base into well-greased 9x13 inch pan.
Bake in a 375° oven for 25 minutes or until golden brown.
Remove from oven and let cool slightly.

Combine water, orange juice, sugar and zest in a saucepan, heat to boiling and let boil gently for 5 minutes.
Add cranberries and boil gently until skins pop, about 5 minutes.
Cool slightly and spread over base.

Place flour, brown sugar, cinnamon and chopped almonds in medium mixing bowl.
Mix butter into dry ingredients with your hands or a pastry blender until mixture is crumbly and texture resembles small peas.
Sprinkle over filling and bake in a 375° oven for 25 minutes.
Cool completely and cut into bars.

We were all so lucky to have known the caring and gracious Pauline. May this recipe always remind her family and her many friends of the happy times they shared with her.

fabulous molasses & 3 ginger cookies

Years ago, the lovely and modest MIchelle shared her mother's recipe for these unique cookies with us. Like a classic gingersnap, these cookies are best dipped in a bit of your afternoon tea! Thanks Michelle!

makes 24 cookies

ingredients

1 ½ cups flour
1 cup brown sugar
1 tsp baking soda
½ tsp salt
1 tsp ginger powder
1 tbsp fresh ginger, peeled and finely grated
2 tsp candied ginger, finely chopped
½ tsp cloves
½ tsp black pepper, finely ground
½ cup shortening, melted and cooled
1 egg
¼ cup molasses
¾ cup large flake oats
¾ cup sugar (for dipping glass in)

method

Mix flour, sugar, baking soda, salt, all gingers, cloves and pepper in a mixing bowl.
Add melted shortening, egg and molasses and beat well.
Add oats until just incorporated.
Scoop cookie batter on to a parchment lined baking sheet by the tablespoon full.
Flatten to ¼ inch height with the bottom of a glass that has been dipped in sugar.
Bake in a 375° oven for 15 minutes or until crisp, switching cookie sheets around in the oven halfway through baking.

Using shortening instead of butter in this cookie recipe will ensure that the cookies hold their shape.

heddle road rhubarb cobbler

Rhubarb is easy to grow in B.C., so if you don't have some growing already, get on it! Otherwise, ask around and friends will be happy to share their bounty. It's also available in the spring at the Kootenay Co-op and the Wednesday Farmer's Market. This recipe has just enough sugar to balance the delicious tartness of the rhubarb.

serves 12

ingredients

base
½ cup butter, cold
¼ cup sugar
1 egg, lightly beaten
2 cups flour
1 tsp baking powder
¼ tsp salt

filling
2 eggs beaten
1 ¾ cups sugar
½ cup butter, melted
1 tsp vanilla
4 cups fresh or frozen rhubarb, chopped into
  one inch pieces
½ cup flour

method

Place butter, sugar, egg, flour, baking powder and salt in mixing bowl and combine with your hands or pastry cutter until mixture is the consistency of small peas.
Press into greased 9x13 inch baking pan, reserving 1 cup of mixture for the topping.

Mix eggs, sugar, melted butter and vanilla until combined.
Toss rhubarb with flour and add to egg mixture.
Spread onto unbaked base.
Sprinkle the reserved base mixture over top of the rhubarb.
Bake at 350° for 45 minutes or until rhubarb mixture is bubbling.

Serve this cobbler straight up with cup of chai for an afternoon snack, or try serving it warm with a scoop of really good vanilla ice cream to turn it into a scrumptious dessert.

gail's pumpkin, walnut & chocolate chip muffins

Everything Gail bakes is fantastic and delicious. Her famous cookies in the previous Whitewater Cookbooks were both huge hits and have filled many lunchbags and backpacks for the last 5 years. She now cooks at a catskiing lodge near Whistler B.C, and those lucky powder hounds get to eat her freshly baked treats daily.

makes 12

ingredients

1 ¾ cups flour
½ tsp allspice
½ tsp cinnamon
½ tsp cloves
1 tsp baking powder
1 tsp baking soda
¾ tsp salt
½ cup butter, room temperature
1 ¼ cup sugar
3 large eggs
1 cup canned pumpkin
1 tsp vanilla
1/3 cup milk
¾ cup chocolate chips (optional)
¾ cup walnuts, chopped
½ cup pumpkin seeds, toasted

method

Pre-heat oven to 350°.
Grease muffin tins.

Sift together flour, allspice, cinnamon, cloves, baking powder, baking soda and salt.
Beat butter until smooth and light.
Mix in sugar until well-combined and then eggs, one at a time.
Beat in pumpkin and vanilla.
Mix dry ingredients into pumpkin mixture alternating with the milk.
Stir in chocolate chips (if using) and walnuts.
Spoon into muffin tins and sprinkle with toasted pumpkin seeds.
Bake for 1 hour.

This recipe is also fantastic baked in a loaf pan and takes 1 hour in the oven at 350°.

banana chocolate icebox cake

An overnight stint in the fridge turns this into a delectable summer picnic cake which travels well by boat. And if by mistake, the dog steps on it, it's quite easy to smooth over the paw print and garnish with another pansy!

serves 8 -10

ingredients

15 oz milk chocolate, chopped into small
   pieces (callebaut is best)
5 large egg yolks, room temperature
pinch of salt
3 cups whipping cream
20 graham wafers
5 ripe bananas, thinly sliced lengthwise
whipped cream for garnish

method

Place chocolate in heatproof bowl.
Place yolks and pinch of salt in another heatproof bowl.
Bring whipping cream to a simmer over low heat in medium saucepan.
Slowly pour warm cream into egg yolks, whisking constantly.
Return cream and egg mixture to saucepan and set over medium low heat.
Cook, stirring constantly until mixture is thick enough to coat the back of a wooden spoon, about 8 minutes. Do not let the mixture come to a boil.
Pour cream and egg mixture over the chopped chocolate and stir until chocolate is smooth and melted.
Refrigerate until thick, about 4 hours, stirring occasionally.

Line a loaf pan with plastic film.
Spread 1 cup of the chocolate mixture evenly into the bottom of the loaf pan.
Top with a layer of graham wafers, trimmed to fit.
Spread 1/2 cup of chocolate mixture on top of graham wafers and cover with a layer of sliced bananas.
Top bananas with another 1/2 cup of chocolate. Add another layer of graham wafers.
Repeat with remaining chocolate, bananas and graham wafers until you reach the top of the pan. Finish with graham wafers.
Cover with plastic film and refrigerate overnight.The next day, uncover and invert on to serving platter. Remove bottom layer of plastic film.
Garnish with whipping cream and edible flowers or mint.

Icebox cake can be refrigerated for up to two days.

sean's simple apple crisp

My little brother Sean has inherited the family cooking gene and takes pride in using fresh, local ingredients to produce this outstanding yet very simple apple crisp. Everyone should have a bomber apple crisp recipe in their life...and a brother like Sean!

serves 6

ingredients

¹⁄₂ cup quick oats
¹⁄₂ cup flour
¹⁄₂ cup brown sugar
¹⁄₂ tsp cinnamon
¹⁄₂ tsp nutmeg
¹⁄₂ cup cold butter, diced

7 tart apples, peeled, cored and sliced (we like macintosh or granny smith)

method

Combine dry ingredients in a mixing bowl.
Add butter pieces to bowl and with your fingers or a pastry cutter, lightly mix butter into dry ingredients until mixture resembles small peas.

Place apples in a buttered 8x8 inch baking dish and cover with crust mixture.
Bake in a 350° oven for 45 minutes or until crispy and golden brown.
Serve with good quality vanilla ice cream.

To make this your own signature fruit crisp, you can add cranberries or rhubarb or even italian plums when they are in season.

shelley sorensen's mom's cheesecake

There are a few classic desserts that everyone is tempted to try their hand at and this should be one of them. Shelley's mom Anita, a long time caterer, made this succulent vanilla cheesecake countless times. We guarantee that you can produce this perfect dessert.

makes one 9 inch springform pan

ingredients

crust
2 cups graham crumbs
3 tbsp sugar
¼ cup sesame seeds, untoasted
dash of cinnamon
4 tbsp butter, melted

cheesecake layer
two 8 oz packages of regular cream cheese,
  room temperature
½ cup sugar
1 tsp vanilla
2 eggs, room temperature, whisked

top layer
2 cups sour cream
3 tbsp sugar
1 tsp vanilla

method

crust
Mix together all ingredients until well combined.
Press into a well-greased springform pan, using the back of a spoon to form the crust, covering the bottom and three quarters up the sides.
Bake in a 325° oven for 5 minutes.
Remove from oven and let cool for 10 minutes.

cheesecake layer
Beat cream cheese in a food processor or with an electric hand mixer, until very smooth.
Add sugar and vanilla and beat again.
Add whisked eggs slowly, until just mixed.
Pour into cooled crust and bake in a 325° oven for 35-40 minutes until just set. When pan is jiggled, the cheesecake should just move ever so slightly.
Remove from oven, but leave oven on, let cool for 10 minutes and spread top layer on.

top layer
Whisk together sour cream, sugar and vanilla, until well mixed.
Spread carefully on to slightly cooled cheesecake.
Bake for 5-10 minutes or until top layer is set when pan is slightly jiggled.
Turn off oven and let cheesecake cool for about 45 minutes, leaving the door partially open
Remove cake, cool completely and refrigerate before serving.
Serve the cake with seasonal berries.

Cheesecake tops often crack and this is because they are cooled too quickly. By leaving the cake in the oven to cool gradually, the cracking will be avoided.

145

the perfect pie crust

Boost your culinary self-image instantly with the success you will surely achieve by producing perfect pie crusts with this recipe. Choose one of the two perfect fillings and you will have pie pride!

makes enough pastry for 2 single 9 inch pie shells

ingredients

2 cups flour
1 ¼ cups Crisco shortening, cold
½ tsp salt
1 tsp sugar
⅓ cup fresh orange juice, juice and pulp, cold

method

Place flour, shortening, salt and sugar in a medium bowl.
Work with your fingers or a pastry cutter, mixing shortening into flour mix until it resembles a bowl full of crumbs the size of small peas.
Add ½ of the orange juice.
Work into crumb mixture and then gradually add the last half of the orange juice until the whole mix just sticks together when you squeeze it in a ball.
Divide dough into two pieces (if you are only making one single crust pie, you can freeze the other piece).
Roll out into a round slightly larger than your pie plate on a lightly floured work surface.
Lift into pie plate, trimming extra off with a sharp knife, just past the edge of the pie plate.
Crimp the edges every ½ inch, all the way around.

For some reason even the most enthusiastic baker seems to hesitate before tackling pie pastry. Approach this easy pie crust method with confidence, paying particular attention to the temperature of the shortening and how much you handle the dough. When you have your hands in there too long, your body temperature will warm up the dough, causing the pie crust to lose flakiness. The less fussing, the better. It's easy as pie!

For 2 perfect fillings, see page 148.

...with 2 perfect fillings

We don't think there exists a more perfect accompaniment to a tub of really good vanilla ice cream or softly whipped cream!

makes filling for 1 pie each

ingredients

liz's pumpkin pie filling
2 tsp cinnamon
1 ½ tsp fresh ginger, peeled and grated
¾ tsp ground nutmeg
½ tsp cloves
2 eggs, slightly beaten in a large bowl
¼ tsp salt
1 cup sugar
1 ⅓ cups whipping cream
⅓ cup half and half cream
1 ½ cups pumpkin, canned (398 ml size)

pecan pie filling
3 eggs
1 cup light or golden corn syrup
1 tbsp butter, melted
⅛ tsp salt
¼ tsp cinnamon
1 tsp vanilla
½ cup white sugar
1 cup pecans, toasted and chopped coarsely

method

liz's pumpkin pie filling
Whisk cinnamon, ginger, nutmeg and cloves into slightly beaten eggs.
Combine salt and sugar and add to egg mixture.
Combine whipping cream and half and half cream and whisk into egg mixture.
Add pumpkin and whisk until smooth.
Pour into the unbaked pie shell.
Bake on middle rack in a 425° oven for 15 minutes.
Reduce oven heat to 325° and bake for another 40-50 minutes, until filling is set or skewer inserted comes out clean. At 25 minutes of baking time, move pies to lower rack in oven so the pie crusts get "bottom heat" and bake through evenly.
Remove from oven and let cool completely before slicing.

pecan pie filling
Beat eggs slightly in a large bowl.
Add corn syrup and melted butter and whisk until well mixed.
Add salt, cinnamon, vanilla and sugar and whisk mixture again until well incorporated.
Add the pecans and stir until just mixed in.
Pour into unbaked pie shell.
Bake in a 400° oven for 15 minutes.
Reduce oven heat to 325° and bake for 45 minutes or until pie is set. You can tell it's set if the filling remains firm when you lightly jiggle the pan.
Cool completely before serving.

Finish off your Thanksgiving dinner with these pies. For turkey tips and Mikes Famous Stuffing, see page 107.

lovely's fall apple almond torte

Piled high with juicy apples, topped with a crunchy almond crust, there lies a hidden delicacy on the bottom of this bountiful cake from our dear gf, "Lovely Linda". Enjoy it, German style, for afternoon coffee!

makes one 9" springform pan - serves 8

ingredients

crust
1 cup flour
1 tsp baking powder
1 pinch salt
1 tsp vanilla
1 tsp lemon zest
$\frac{1}{4}$ cup sugar
$\frac{1}{2}$ cup butter, cold
1 egg

torte
3 lbs. apples (granny smith are best), peeled, cored and cut into 1 inch chunks
$\frac{1}{2}$ lemon, juice and zest of
$\frac{1}{3}$ cup raisins
5 tbsp butter, melted
$\frac{1}{2}$ cup sugar
1 tbsp flour
$\frac{1}{2}$ cup almond paste or marzipan*
3 tbsp whipping cream
1$\frac{1}{2}$ tbsp honey
$\frac{3}{4}$ cup almonds, sliced

*available at Ellison's Market, seasonally – if you can't find it, see recipe below:

almond paste*
1 $\frac{1}{2}$ cup ground almonds, toasted lightly in oven and cooled
1 $\frac{1}{2}$ cup icing sugar, sift
1 tsp almond extract
1 egg white, unbeaten

method

crust
Pulse flour, baking powder, salt, vanilla, zest, sugar, 2 tbsp of the butter and egg together in food processor until a ball forms, about 2 minutes.
Remove from processor, knead a few times on a floured surface, shape into a flat disc and let rest in fridge for $\frac{1}{2}$ hour.

torte
Toss apples with lemon juice and zest, raisins, butter and sugar in a heavy bottomed sauce pan.
Heat on medium heat for 7-8 minutes and then let cool.
Stir in flour and combine.
Roll out rested dough on a floured surface to a 12 inch circle and then line springform or tarte pan with dough.
Crumble almond paste onto the dough.
Fill with cooled apple mixture.
Mix remaining butter, cream and honey together and boil for 2 minutes.
Add almond slices and boil another minute.
Pour mixture over apple cake evenly.
Bake for 40 minutes at 350°.

Cool completely, remove from pan and serve with vanilla tinged whipped cream or homemade ice cream.

almond paste
Mix almond paste ingredients in the food processor and whiz on high until well blended and forming a ball, about 2 minutes.
Wrap in plastic film and store in fridge until needed.

If you can't find almond paste in the stores any time of year but Christmas, here is an easy recipe to make your own.

treeplanters eatmore bars

Marianne B., awesome mother and local cookie maker, used to make these bars for ravenous treeplanters and now for the crew of kids that is often at her house. They taste just like the real thing!

makes 32 bars

ingredients

1 cup golden corn syrup
2 cups chocolate chips
$\frac{1}{2}$ cup smooth organic peanut butter
2 cups rice crispies or quick oats*
2 cups unsalted peanuts, toasted and
  chopped
$\frac{1}{2}$ tsp salt

*we prefer rice crispies, but oats, of course, are healthier.

method

Place corn syrup, chocolate chips and peanut butter in a saucepan and melt together on low heat, stirring often, until melted and mixed well.
Transfer to large bowl.
Add rice crispies (or oats), peanuts and salt.
Stir with a wooden spoon until well mixed.
Press into a greased 9x13 inch pan.
Cool completely and cut into bars.

A local performance athlete researched the comparative nutritional values of an Eatmore bar vs. a Power bar and concluded that the two were equivalent in their energy delivery. So make these instead and take them along for great fuel!

laura's caramel corn

This tasty, fun snack is reminiscent of the popular "Kettle Corn". Your kids can make it and then take it in a big tin to a movie watching overnighter with their friends. Of course, it's also great for us big kids as we like snacking on it while watching the Oscars! Thanks to the gorgeous Laura for sharing this recipe.

makes 8-10 cups

ingredients

8 cups popped popcorn ($\frac{1}{2}$ cup raw kernels)
$\frac{3}{4}$ cup almonds (whole and toasted)
$\frac{3}{4}$ cup whole pecans, toasted
$\frac{1}{2}$ cup butter
1 cup white sugar
$\frac{1}{4}$ cup golden corn syrup
$\frac{1}{2}$ tsp salt
$\frac{1}{4}$ tsp baking soda
$\frac{1}{2}$ tsp vanilla

method

Preheat oven to 350°.
Place popcorn in a really big bowl.
Add toasted nuts and combine.
Place butter, sugar, corn syrup and salt in a saucepan and bring to a boil at low heat.
Boil for 8 minutes, stirring only once.
Remove from heat and stir in baking soda and vanilla.
Pour over popcorn and nut mixture while hot and toss with wooden spoons until well coated.
Spread on parchment lined baking sheet and bake for 15-20 minutes.
Stir with a spatula once while baking.
Let cool and break into bite-size chunks.
Store in airtight containers or cookie tins.

Toasting improves the flavour and texture of nuts immeasurably. It's easy, just spread them on a baking sheet and toast in a 350° oven for 10 minutes. We suggest using a timer though, as nuts can burn REALLY fast when unattended!

mia's warm gingerbread pudding cake

Way up in the Purcell mountains above Kaslo lies a gorgeous ski touring operation called Powder Creek. Inside the kitchen there can be found an even more gorgeous gal named Mia who serves this warm and cozy pudding cake to many contented, rosy cheeked powder skiers. Mia's speciality lies in producing exceptionally beautiful meals for all and never missing a day to lay down some sweet powder lines herself! A consummate Kootenay girl, Mia is adored by all of us lucky friends.

serves 8

ingredients

1 ¼ cups flour
1 tsp ground ginger
¾ tsp baking soda
½ tsp cinnamon
¼ tsp nutmeg
¼ tsp allspice
¼ tsp cloves
¼ tsp salt

¼ cup butter, room temperature
¼ cup sugar
1 egg, room temperature, beaten slightly
½ cup molasses
½ cup warm water
¾ cup brown sugar
1 ½ cups hot water
5 tbsp butter, room temperature

method

Preheat oven to 350°.

Grease a 9 inch oval oven proof baking dish, or an 8x8 inch glass baking dish well with butter or pam-type spray.
Place flour, ginger, baking soda, cinnamon, nutmeg, allspice, cloves and salt in a mixing bowl and whisk together until combined.
Beat butter and sugar until well combined and then add beaten egg until just blended.
Combine molasses and warm water together in glass measuring cup.
Mix flour mixture into butter mixture alternately with molasses mixture blending well.
Transfer to prepared baking dish and sprinkle with the brown sugar.
Combine 1 ½ cups hot water and 5 tbsp butter in a glass measuring cup and carefully pour over the top of the batter. There will be a lot of liquid on top!
Bake until crackled looking, 35-40 minutes.
Remove from oven and let cool for at least 10 minutes.
Scoop warm pudding cake into individual bowls and serve with whipped cream or your favourite vanilla ice cream.

Feel free to make this pudding cake earlier in the day, then just quickly re-heat it, to bring it back to a fresh "out of the oven" warm dessert just before serving...

index

Barb

Sheri

Mia

Lovely

Blake

Lisa

Nathan

Shelley

Pat

Liz

thanks!
for sharing

Ralf

Susi

Mar

Bernice

Marilyn

Michele

Ta

Cathy

Barbie

Sue

Marcia

Jane

Annie

Jann

Mike

Tempy

Sean

Marianne

Kim

Gail

Monica

Laura

Fiona

Petra

Emmy

O

Daphne